ASIA MINOR

ASIA MINOR

WITH

160 PICTURES IN PHOTOGRAVURE

8 COLOUR PLATES

AND INTRODUCTION BY

MAXIM OSWARD

WILLIAM MORROW AND COMPANY

TRANSLATED FROM THE GERMAN
BY NORMA DEANE

© M. OSWARD MUNICH
AND THAMES AND HUDSON LONDON 1957
PRINTED IN GERMANY BY BELSERDRUCK STUTTGART
THE PHOTOGRAPHER'S ASSISTANT: PETER REINSTORFF

CONTENTS

AWAY BACK IN TURKEY . . .!

Books have been written and volumes of photographs published covering almost every country in the world: every people, every newly-discovered corner of the globe, even whole continents have been brought nearer to us in this way. Countless authors in every known language have taken us on journeys, to desolate mountain peaks in the East and to lonely forgotten creeks in Iceland, deep into the steaming African jungle and up into the high hills of the South American Andes. But one region still remains shrouded in an enigmatic silence — a region on the threshold of Europe, from which our continent has derived not merely an abundance of wealth, knowledge and beauty, but also the gift of marvellous philosophies and age-old wonders, formed by centuries of tradition or wrought in stone. That region is Asia Minor.

Possibly we do show some interest if, say, newspaper reports tell of archaeologists searching for Noah's Ark in the area around Mount Ararat, at 5580 feet the highest peak in Asia Minor. But what do we know about the country where the Turks live . . .? We have a vague recollection that Byzantium once ruled over that empire, and that it fell before the invading Asiatic hordes: we know that the armies of the Crusaders marched through Asia Minor towards the Holy Land, and that a brilliant German named Schliemann discovered the site of the ancient city of Troy. When Europeans wear Phrygian caps, how many among them are aware that these same Phrygians set up their capital, Gordion, in the Anatolian highlands, near the site of the present-day Turkish capital, Ankara? Here it was that Alexander the Great showed the Phrygians how and by what means he would subdue Asia Minor, when the knot in the harness of the Phrygian king Gordius was presented for him to untie, and he cut through it with his sword. So Gordion was down there where Ankara stands to-day? Yes, away back in Turkey . . .!

Travelling across this eastern land-bridge, we find our interest grow day by day, as we trace in the carved stone almost six thousand years of history. The fantastic gods worshipped by long-vanished nations come to light; heroes of classical times and their gods emerge from the shadows of the past; and on every hand we come upon familiar names in history, until we realise with astonishment just how often we mentioned Asia Minor before, and how little the name really meant for us until now. The names of ancient peoples, legendary figures, emperors and kings, poets and philosophers, gods — and God — spring from the soil of this blessed land. Conquerors in their brazen armour and Apostles in their cowled habits took the peoples of Asia Minor by storm. Picture writings, cuneiform inscriptions, Greek and Roman tablets all tell of vanished civilisations which flourished when our own was yet unformed, and whose influence is still felt in our modern world. A single book of pictures is not enough to show all this. In one volume we can only try to give some indication of the whole, and to choose one or two focal points from the enormous mass of available material. This means that the Asia Minor of to-day will only be glimpsed as it were incidentally, and that the emphasis must be laid on documentary photographs. At the risk of anticipating various events, one is sorely tempted to reel off a list of famous names connected in past ages with Asia Minor. And even then the list must be confined to the most illustrious among them.

About 2600 B. C. the mythical king of Accad, Saigon I, marched towards Cilicia, as did the Babylonian Queen Semiramis in 810 B.C. Homer of the legends is said to have been born at Ephesus. The Persian kings, Xerxes and Cyrus, passed through at the head of their respective armies, the latter defeating the rich Lydian king, Croesus, in 546 B.C. About 525 B.C. Xenophon led his Greeks to the shores of the Black Sea, where they settled. Heraclitus of Ephesus (523—475 B.C.) and Herodotus of Halicarnassus (484—425 B.C.) dwelt on the west coast of Asia Minor; Diogenes (414—323 B.C.) was born in Sinope on the Black Sea; and Aristotle of Stagira (384—322 B.C.) was active in these parts. Here, too, Alexander the Great defeated Darius II; Antony and Cleopatra visited Tarsus on their wedding journey; Mithridates was defeated by Sulla and Lucullus; and Pompey, Caesar and Vespasian led their cohorts through the land. The Apostle John and Mary the Mother of Jesus made their way back to Ephesus, their native town in Asia Minor, after the death of Our Lord, bringing with them many Christians fleeing from Palestine, and Luke and Mary Magdalene followed in their footsteps. Paul was born in the city of Tarsus; and the Emperor Diocletian, Constantine the Great, Julian the Apostate, Theodosius the Great, Justinian and Haroun-al-Raschid have all left their mark on Asia Minor. Genghis Khan and his Mongol hordes swept through the land, which one hundred and fifty years later was ravaged by Tamerlane (the Mongol leader Timur Lenk) who distracted the attention of the Sultan Bayezid Yilderim (the Thunderbolt) from the siege of Constantinople, and afterwards defeated him at the Battle of Ankara in 1402. Frederick I — Barbarossa — was drowned near Tarsus, and Geoffroi de Bouillon, Richard Coeur-de-Lion and the Babenbergs came as Crusaders to Asia Minor. The Osman Sultan Mehemet II, the conqueror, captured Constantinople: Suleiman the Magnificent stood with his armies before the gates of Vienna; and in our own times we must not forget that great statesman, Kemal Atatürk, hailed by the Turks as the father of their nation. This is only a small, albeit impressive selection; but it serves to conjure up from the past a great civilisation which all our European learning cannot discredit. The cultures of Persia and Mesopotamia, and of Greece and Rome, as well as the influence of both Judaism and Christianity, have all entered our common way of life. The East has not merely given us tea, myrrh and incense, and the origins of philosophy, astronomy and history. The concept of a monotheistic doctrine first took root and spread in Asia Minor, and was established, expanded and purified in the Councils of Nicaea, Chalcedon and Ephesus, before going on to conquer Europe and the world.

"Ex Oriente Lux"

"All light comes from the East!"

This Latin saying is not designed simply to emphasise for us the familiar astronomical phenomenon of the sun's daily appearance in the morning sky, but to remind us that for thousands of years men have recognised that all human knowledge has its roots in the Near and Far East. "Ex Oriente Lux" is equally valid for modern man, who is still unconsciously reaping the benefits of oriental thinking. Despite his own intellectual development, the European has for centuries taken account of this light from the East, always without quite realising the strength of that light. It appears in the most diverse and, on occasion, the most mystical guises, and modern man's humdrum intellect often cannot see the central force underlying the outward trappings. The eastern tenet "all being is spirit" is opposed to the European's rationalist dogma "what does not exist, cannot be", and oriental meditation — the striving for one-ness with the Absolute, as practised to this day by the Turks — is incompatible with western modes of thought.

The East forms a vast and varied part of the Globe, with the Near East lying athwart the eastern Mediterranean at the gateway of ancient Europe, its northern wing, Asia Minor, extending as far as the Bosporus, and its southern wing, North Africa, stretching along the southern Mediterranean to the Pillars of Hercules. This North African strip and the land-bridge formed by Asia Minor has until now been the area where the influence of East on West has been most strongly felt; and European culture in its turn flowed back along these two 'wings' towards the East. But there were natural geopolitical boundaries which ensured that, though intellectual relationships were possible, physical contacts were of a transitory nature and stopped short where the frontiers crossed. Oil and water cannot mix. Nevertheless, the stream of light flowed back and forth, and, as the centuries passed, there grew up a common civilisation in these boundary regions, which radically affected the structure of our own western culture. It is fascinating to set out from these demarcation lines and try to trace separately the various factors contributed by each side to the common civilisation. The first major divisions are naturally those of space and time, and while the space was presumably always constant, in time we must go back for thousands of years, lengthening our own short life-span with a time-telescope in order to re-live past history. We realise immediately, however, that a third factor lurks behind those of time and space, a factor which we must consider, which defies comprehension, but which by its constant presence forces itself upon our attention — the Ineffable, the Spirit of the East, older than the oldest myth, deeper than the deepest hidden secrets of the world, springing from the very source of creation.

Until the last century, when the man-made Suez Canal opened a new route from the Mediterranean to the Red Sea, Asia Minor was the natural bridge linking East and West. It guarded the rich trade-routes, along which passed an endless stream of caravans bringing the costly luxuries and fabulous wealth of the Orient to the cold and covetous merchant-princes of the West. But as they transferred the precious freight from the camels' backs to their own horses and ships, the Europeans absorbed at the same time many of the mystical legends of the East. The *Arabian Nights' Entertainment* and the Turkish lyrics of Goethe's *Westöstlicher Divan* (divan being the Turkish word for poetry) are not the only example of this literary contact. The Greeks, too, owed much of their mythology to the cults of the Hittite tribes of Asia Minor.

Asia Minor, the area with which this book is concerned, forms a small part of the great continent of Asia, to which it may well have given its name. Its westernmost point on the Bosporus lies on the threshold of Eastern Europe, and its eastern boundary is guarded by the high peak of Mount Ararat. Its shores are washed in the north by the Black Sea, in the west by the Bosporus, the Sea of Marmora, the Dardanelles (the ancient Hellespont) and the Aegean, and in the south by the White Sea — the eastern Mediterranean. Three high mountain ranges traverse the country from east to west, so that the interior, known as Anatolia, or the Motherland, is high, rugged and somewhat inaccessible. Asia Minor, with its rich and fertile regions in the west and south, is a land of deep unrest. Since the world began it has been ravaged by earthquakes; rivers have become silted up so that coastal towns have gradually receded into the hinterland and thus been stripped of their former importance; and in some areas erosion has played such havoc with the soft stone that the landscape is reminiscent of the surface of the moon. But all round her coasts she is guarded by her many different seas . . .

"Allahi ekbèr!" remarked an officer of the Turkish Navy to a fellow-passenger, as they sat in the swiftly-moving, heaving ferry-boat plying between Europe and Asia, across the Bosporus. As he spoke, his rapt gaze was fixed on the enormous surging breakers which Allah was at that moment directing towards them from the Sea of Marmora. The officer's little neighbour looked at him scornfully. He was a Jew from Constantinople, and though the Jews may be the best dealers in that great centre of international trade, they are no sailors. He had probably often travelled on the little ferry between Istanbul and Kadiköy; but the Lodos, the great south wind, rarely blew as strongly as it was doing that day, and all the passengers were aware of the danger. On board the little boat silence reigned, as they listened to the waves crashing against the timbers of the hull and drowning the noise of the engine. A sardonic glint appeared in the eyes of the Jewish trader, as he repeated "Allahi ekbèr!" — "God is great!" The Turkish officer looked down at him with an expression of impassive dignity. Suddenly, a gigantic wave shook the whole ship! The little boat held its course, rode the wave, but would surely disappear the next minute under the mass of swirling water. It was enough to make even the oldest water rat desert! There was a momentary lull, in which the trader from Constantinople was heard to remark wryly to the Turk: "Yes indeed, my friend, God is great — but the ship is small!" In an instant all the dignity and anxiety were swept away in a burst of laughter, while the ferry-boat slipped into the sheltered waters of the little harbour at Kadiköy, once the ancient city of Chalcedon. Allàhu alèm! This hot south wind usually blows itself out in three days at the most, and then the Byzantine sun shines again in all its former splendour. The deep blue waters of the Bosporus flow into the calm, sparkling Sea of Marmora as though the storm had never been. Here stands Byzantium-Constantinople-Istanbul, on the eastern edge of Europa, while on the opposite shore the red blossoms of the Judas-trees mark the gateway to the Orient. It makes a peaceful scene, this great international harbour lying on either side of the sea-lane of the Bosporus. Here West and East touch, intersect, and mingle briefly, for complete unity is impossible. As the Bosporus flows for ever from the Black Sea into the Sea of Marmora, down through the Dardanelles into the Aegean, until the 'black waters' finally merge with the blue of the Mediterranean, so the fertile wave of culture moves ceaselessly from East to West and, according to ancient law, back again from West to East. So it was, and so it is to-day, for the Cross has allied itself to the Crescent.

Cross and Crescent! What historic memories they bring to mind. But these must wait until later. The foreigner on Byzantine soil is struck at the outset by a division between the two worlds. Even after a short time in Istanbul, if he is not entirely immersed in the historical aspect of the city, he will become very much aware of this cleavage, which is inherent in everything, in the people and in their thinking. The reason is that from its very beginnings, Byzantium, the easternmost city of Western Europe, was really oriental in character. Yet all the peoples of Asia Minor who came flooding into the metropolis, and all those who attacked her, regarded her as belonging to the West. Though in this modern technical age Orient and Occident may grow daily nearer geographically, spiritually they are as far apart as ever. And so, after some initial fluctuation, both Cross and Crescent stopped short at this natural frontier, and came to terms. They can never become one!

It was originally planned to produce a book of photographs entitled *The Land of the Turks*, and it would undoubtedly have been a simpler matter to travel through modern Turkey in a diesel-engined truck, photographing the more obvious aspects of Asia Minor. There would certainly have been no scarcity of material.

Years have passed since I first stood on the western shores of the Bosporus and looked across at the continent on the other side. So that was Asia Minor! A constant stream of jaunty small craft, long-boats and ferry-boats, made it easy for the stranger to cross the straits from Istanbul, ancient capital of the Osman Sultans on the eastern edge of Europe. But the great city on the Golden Horn still preserves all the glamour of a metropolis, though she is no longer the capital of Turkey.

The brilliant statesman Atatürk, who understood the character of his people better than any other, forcibly deprived the city of her proud title, and the present-day Ankara, formerly Ankyra, which has stood for thousands of years on the high Anatolian plateau of Galatia, became the capital city of the smaller Turkey which we know to-day. It has always been a characteristic of great statesmen that their acts have constantly been guided by a sure knowledge of the strength and weakness of their own people. This is not mere lip-service to the great man of Turkey, but the recognition of a central truth which emerges from the history of Asia Minor.

He may well have been misled in his impulsive haste to prove the relationships of the Osmans, Turks and Seljuks to the Accadians, Sumerians and Hittites; but it is certain that the Turkish people was made up not of intellectuals, merchants and seafarers, but of soldiers, tax-collectors and the Sultans' government officials. Atatürk saw that the real Turks were not those who had built up the city of Constantinople into a world trade centre which remained a stronghold of the western powers, with their famous 'concessions', right up to the end of the first world war.

Nevertheless, the transfer of the seat of government from the great port of Constantinople — even though it weakened the strong European influence exerted on Turkish affairs by that city — to its present secure central position in the Anatolian highlands, was a step which could have been taken only by a popular demagogue! Ankara lies in the heart of Anatolia, cradle of so many ancient tribes and *alma mater* to the whole of Europe.

The second of our demarcation lines lies along the River Halys, to-day the Kizil-Irmak or Red River, which flows for more than 700 miles down through the hill country towards the Black Sea. Even in Roman times it was regarded as the frontier of Asia, and on its banks there lay the two great kingdoms of the Hittites, with their capital city of Hattusa, and the land of their conquerors, the Phrygians, whose capital was at Gordion. There, too, after the first world war, rose the new Kemalite-Turkish Republic.

The great arc cut by the Halys divides central Asia Minor into two parts.

Is it chance, or fate, that all the kingdoms of this land bounded by the eastern Mediterranean, the Aegean, the Sea of Marmora and the Black Sea, were established in the central uplands, and not in the coastal plains? Hattusil, king of the Hittites, though besieged by the mighty armies of his enemies, could not be dislodged from his capital Hattusa, and even dared to defy the widow of the great Pharaoh Tutenkhamen, when she desired one of his sons for her husband and consort. How much wiser he was to remain in the security of his mountains than to scatter his forces far and wide in an attempt to defend the coastal plains of his kingdom. His grandson Marsilis in all probability allied himself with the kings of 'Ahhija' on the Aegean (surely the Hittite version of 'Achaei', one of the principal tribes which took part in the Trojan war), and reigned from 1334 to 1306 B.C., that is to say, about the time of that great campaign. His power was so great that he not only took successful punitive measures against the rebellious city of Aleppo, but also annexed Babylon as a proof of strength. But he, too, always returned to his mountain fortress of Hattusa. What of the Phrygians, the conquerors of these Hittites? They had also established their capital in the mountains, to the west of Ankara.

The Turks are a nation of soldiers: so, too, were the Hittites. Could we not see in this a link or a parallel?

When one has spent several years living among the Turks, the wide regions of Anatolia gradually become more accessible, until at last the way is opened, and one embarks on a voyage of discovery. The explorer sets about his task at his own risk. It is not merely that he is entering a vast unknown territory; but he is at the same time confronted with five or six thousand years of past history. Asia Minor strikes the European with awe and wonder, for among the Turks of to-day he finds both the descendants of the great leader Ertoghrul, who led his handful of warriors over the Caucasus towards the south, and those of the Sumerians, Accadians, Hittites, Hurrians, Assyrians, Achaeans, Greeks and Galatians, all combining in the new race.

The bold and courageous Alexander the Great proved the might of the Macedonian armies by overrunning the kingdom of Lydia and advancing through Phrygia as far as the Halys, into our third zone, Cilicia. He followed the river's course, leaving the battlefields of Issus and Gaugamela to mark his passage, pursued the Persians to the very gates of their capital, Persepolis, and pressed on to the banks of the Indus, staking his all on the fulfilment of his grandiose plans for the conquest of the East. But this was not to be. He died of a mysterious fever, and his generals attempted to establish little states on the Mediterranean coast, and to salvage what they could for themselves and their Macedonians from the ruins of Alexander's grand design. Though the unified civilisation of Macedonia, Greece and Persia which Alexander had striven to create did in fact form a bulwark against the oncoming wave of arabic culture, it remained a small outpost in that vast foreign land.

To this day fair-haired Arab children with blue Macedonian eyes can be seen in parts of Syria and Cilicia, and one finds French-speaking 'Greeks' who have long ago abandoned the Greek tongue. They are descended from the inhabitants of the Seleucid kingdom of Syria, founded by Seleucus Nicator, one of Alexander's generals, where the Macedonian-Persian culture was preserved for centuries until at last the Romans conquered Antiochus IV and his Greek allies. In 64 B.C., Pompey subdued the Black Sea kingdoms and the remains of the kingdom of Seleucus. This third frontier zone is known as 'the fertile crescent', stretching from Mesopotamia through Tarsus and Seleucia (the Silifke of to-day) and forming what must surely be Asia Minor's Garden of Eden. It seems incredible that Adam should have been born elsewhere — and is not 'Adam' the Turkish word for a man or a human being? The long curve begins in Ur, touches Antioch (Antakya) and then Alexandretta-Iscanderoon, sweeps through Tarsus, Mersin and Pompeiopolis to end at Corycus, near Seleucia and Anemurium (Anamour) facing the Island of Cyprus.

This is the ancient Cilicia of the Bible, with Tarsus, city of the tentmakers, as its centre, and here the famous Cilician Gates guard the entrance to the central regions of Anatolia. Through these gates came the armies of the Third Crusade under Frederick Barbarossa; and here they halted and turned back towards Europe. They never reached the Holy Land, for they lost their leader near Tarsus, city of the Apostle Paul, whose name is known throughout Europe. It was through these Cilician Gates that so many armies passed, eager to conquer Palestine or Europe.

To the west of Tarsus lies a fruitful plain rich in orange groves, and still further west an inaccessible peninsula juts out into the sea towards Cyprus, separating western Anatolia, the Ionia of ancient Greece in the Aegean, from the earthly paradise in the south-east, which follows the coast down towards the south, across the battlefield of Issus and on to the high mountain ranges of the Lebanon and Anti-Lebanon. And there we come upon the biblical Antioch, sheltered by hills, city of the Apostles! What more historic boundary could be drawn? For, this region was famous among all the peoples of the Near East, Mesopotamia, Egypt and Europe.

This line encloses what was once the Roman province of Syria; but the region is remarkable not so much for its historical interest, great as that is, as for its fertility and its quite extraordinary beauty. This paradise on the shores of the Mediterranean, hailed by the French as surpassing the Riviera, because more unspoiled, offers a wonderful vista of the ancient world, the cities of the Bible and the beginnings of European civilisation. Here we can dream as Adam dreamed . . . here lay the antique city of Corycus. The stranger, when confronted by the villas of the Greek,

Seleucid and Roman aristocracy, traces of which can still be seen amid the luxuriant groves of yew, by the huge aqueduct of the Emperor Vespasian or the cool cave-dwellings of the Roman officers under Mount Lebanon, suddenly realises what a spell this land must once have cast on the rest of the world.

At the end of our wide curve we come on the Aegean coastlands, often ravaged by earthquakes. The fourth stage in our pilgrimage begins by the cedar-clad slopes of Gazipasha, and the road leads through Alanya, Side, Attaleia (Antalya) and Halicarnassus, across the Meander to Ephesus. Vineyards and fig groves line our route as we come finally to Smyrna (Izmir) and the Dardanelles. This was no mere Greek colony, but a source of Greek learning, wisdom and inspiration. From the soil of Asia Minor Greece drew her greatest treasures . . . from Cyprus by way of Troy and the Hellespont, the light streamed forth . . .

Until the advent of Atatürk western Anatolia, shattered again and again by disastrous earth-quakes and rebuilt each time with uncanny speed, had been essentially a Greek domain. This is clear from the foundations of Troy, Smyrna, Ephesus, Side and many other towns. And, as though earthquakes were not enough, the region was ravaged by invading armies from Lydia, Persia, Macedonia, Rome and Mongolia. Nevertheless, the Greek strain predominated. It was only after the decline of Byzantium — which began long before that city was captured by the Turks — that the Greeks found themselves bereft both of the strength of their parent country and of the powerful leadership of the Orthodox Church, and they finally lost their contact with their hereditary homeland when their province was annexed by Atatürk at the end of the first world war. Remnants of the Greek population cling to the mainland, while Greece still possesses the islands of the Dodecanese. This marked the tragic end of a civilisation weakened by inbreeding. Nowadays the population of the fertile plains of western Anatolia is predominantly Turkish, apart from the scattered groups we have mentioned: but the contemporary situation in Cyprus is a most striking example of the bitter feelings which to this day exist between Turks and Greeks. And so to the northern sector of Asia Minor, whose boundary extends along the Black Sea from the Bosporus to Trabzon (Trebizond) and eastward to the Caucasus.

Scene of countless battles, buffeted by the storms of the Black Sea, hampered by her lack of safe harbours and her rugged hinterland, this region has not developed to the same extent as the fertile south. To these shores came Xenophon of Athens, pupil of Socrates, general, philosopher and historian, at the head of 10,000 Spartan troops he had led out of northern Babylonia, and in the 6th century B. C. they settled here. From this colony grew the Pontic kingdom whose Persian ruler, Mithridates VI, captured in 110 B. C. Cappadocia and the Greek states on the Black Sea. The backbone of this kingdom, however, was broken by the Roman generals Sulla and Lucullus in the so-called Mithridatic Wars of 74—67 B. C., and in 64 B. C. Pompey the Great finally shattered the remaining power of the dynasty. So the little kingdom in northern Anatolia passed into the Roman Empire to form a part of the Province of Asia . . .

This frontier was constantly invaded by victorious armies from further east. Genghis Khan, great ruler of all the mid-Asiatic, Mongolian, Turkish and Tartar tribes, defeated the combined might of the south Russian princes in 1223 at Kiev, having previously captured Peking, and his armies, carrying all before them, swept down into Asia Minor: but four years later even this great Mongolian Empire had crumbled. Its later ruler, Timurlenk, despite his victory over the Turks at Ankara, was also unable to hold down this region. In the end it was the Turks, who occupied the area under their leader Ertoghrul and allied themselves with their restless kinsmen from Mesopotamia, the Seljuks, who made the final conquest of Anatolia. The country reminded them of their own eastern homeland, and, having won it by perseverance and courage, they proceeded to establish a strong kingdom under their Osman padishahs.

The Russians have never succeeded in crossing this northern frontier, though for a thousand years it has barred their way to the Mediterranean.

Our five zones have not been determined in an arbitrary way. Through the ages all the neighbouring tribes — Assyrians, Medes and Persians, the Balkan peoples, Romans, Christian Crusaders and Russians — have recognised their boundaries. They might be invaded; but they could never be held. That was why the Hittites kept to their mountain fastness, while the plains below were filled with their smaller, vassal states. And that was why Atatürk removed the seat of government to the safety of the central highlands.

Let us return to the Bosporus, whose blue waters separate two continents. For two thousand six hundred years the struggle has gone on at this first frontier of all, and the city has over the centuries been given many different names. The Dorians and Greeks called it Byzantium; the Arabs knew it as Anthusa, City of Prosperity, Home of Bliss (Dar-el-Saadat); and the Romans named it, first Antonia, then Nova Roma and finally Constantinopolis. It was Zarigrad to the Slavs, and now, since the time of Atatürk, the Turks have called it Istanbul, from the Greek phrase meaning 'to the city'. And Anatolia, the Motherland, has watched and waited for thousands of years . . .

Just as in earlier times the mother of the family was the focal point of all society, so the Great Mother ruled in the kingdom of the gods. She was Kupapa, Sun Goddess of the Hittites, central figure in a galaxy of a thousand gods; later she appeared as Cybele, whose orgiastic cult flourished in Anatolia. While these figures are sexless, they are at the same time maternal. It was here, too, that the famous Diana of Ephesus held sway in her golden temple which was one of the wonders of the ancient world, and against her that the first Christians, with Luke as their leader, raised the new and peaceful symbol of the Cross. On the hills above this sacred golden temple of Diana the Great Mother of Christendom was born. Meryemanè, as they call the Mother of Christ, is revered by the Turks, too, for Islam recognises the great Prophet Jesus of Nazareth, and after Christ's death on the Cross she returned to her native hills, accompanied by the young John, there to live out her days on earth.

"Ex Oriente Lux . . .!"

And so at length, after much hesitation, it was decided that the purpose of this book should be to follow these five lines which are so deeply graven on the face of Anatolia; and our three guides on this long journey were the Sun, the Cross and the Crescent.

Now that we have some idea of the country from a geographical and geopolitical point of view, it is the turn of the time telescope, which must help us to cover some five thousand years, that is, from the earliest beginnings of human civilisation right up to the present day.

It seems reasonably certain that until the third millennium B.C. Asia Minor was inhabited by an ancient Dinaric people, speaking a primitive Caucasian language known as Proto-Chattish; and it is conjectured that the Etruscans, who came from south-western Anatolia, were related to this people. Into this already inhabited country came the Sumerians, who extended their power in Mesopotamia between 3,100 and 2,900 B.C. These Sumerians, in 2350, founded the first nation in Babylonian history, and the dynasty of Accad came to exert a powerful influence on the land of Asia Minor. There are still clear traces of the Accadians, and their deity, Zababa, appears frequently in the later Hittite cuneiform inscriptions, testifying to the important consequences of Sargon's invasion of Anatolia. About the same time, the first Indo-Germanic tribes of the Hittites slowly infiltrated into the region and settled there, building small towns, and bringing with them their own Indo-Germanic gods.

In the days of the Sumerians there existed in Turkestan the oldest known tribe of oasis-dwellers, the first Egyptian kingdom with its new capital at Memphis, and the highly developed culture of Crete. In Europe, the civilisation of the Middle Stone Age prevailed. But we must telescope a thousand years to draw these parallels, which are at best only approximate.

While central and northern Europe were still passing through the Neolithic Age, and the famous lake-dwellings were being built in Lake Constance, the Hittites in Asia Minor were laying the foundations of their first great kingdom in 1950 B.C., by grouping together a number of neighbouring city-states. The ruins of Hattusa are still visible near Bogazköy, a mere 105 miles northeast of Ankara. Not far from them stand the carved cliffs of Yazilikaya, where the people came to worship their gods. We shall hear more of them later. This first great empire in Asia Minor survived until 1475 B.C., growing in greatness under Hattusil and his grandson Marsilis I. A new Hittite kingdom arose in 1475 to replace the old, only to fall in 1192 B.C. before the armies of the Phrygians, who likewise sprang from Indo-Germanic stock. The Hittites continued to exist in small city-states; but they intermarried with their conquerors, just as they themselves had long ago intermarried with the original inhabitants of the country.

At this time, too — about 1750 B.C., — the Achaeans were rebuilding the ruined city of Troy, which about 1200 B.C. was to provide the historical background for the 'Iliad'. The Hittites were allies of the Achaeans, a fact often forgotten by the Greek settlers on the west coast of Anatolia, whose ancestors owed a great deal to the fruitfulness of this contact. The highly-developed civilisation of the Hittites, their old-established gods and their political concepts spread across the western plains and left a lasting imprint on the Greek colonies there, without which the flowering of Greek culture would never have taken place. This may sound surprising; but it is to-day a recognised fact. The Etruscans travelled westward from Asia Minor and became the preceptors of Rome, while the mature civilisation of the Hittites foreshadowed the golden age of Athens. It was at the king's court in Hattusa that Greek youths first learned the classic art of chariot racing, which they brought back with them when they returned to their own country. The Phrygian kingdom which arose from the ruins of the mighty Hittite empire in turn gave place to that of the Lydians, a people who apparently had some kinship with the Hittites, according to philological research. Their capital was Sardis. Under their famous king, Croesus, the Lydians were defeated and annihilated in 546 B.C. by the Persians, led by Cyrus. Herodotus tells us that the Lydians were a highly-civilised people, a statement borne out by extant Lydian tombstones. Their kingdom was governed for the next two centuries by a Persian satrap, and it was not until the victorious phalanxes of Alexander the Great overran Asia Minor that both the Persian colonies and the Greek settlers regained their freedom. Alexander was determined to combine his own Greek and Macedonian culture with that of Mesopotamia, and to raise this triple civilisation to new heights in one great common empire.

By 1000 B.C. the Bronze Age had given way in Europe to the Iron Age. Between 1000 and 500 B.C. the influence of Etrusco-Greek culture was all-powerful in Italy, and from 500 B.C. the dissemination of Greek and Roman learning began, spreading out from various centres in southern Europe, while to the west the Celts and Iberians were gathering their strength. On their expeditions to the Black Sea the Dorians founded Byzantium, about 660 B.C. The mythical Byzes, a son of the sea-god Poseidon, gave his name to this city on the Bosporus which succeeded Troy. Like Rome, Byzantium was built on seven hills, and again like the eternal city, was coveted by many conquerors. No other city has for two thousand years been so repeatedly attacked. It has survived twenty-four sieges and been captured six times, by the Greeks, the Romans, the Crusaders, the Greek Palaeologues and finally by the Turks; it has withstood attacks by the Persians, Slavs and Arabs. Byzantium and Rome became the two great strongholds of the Christian Church, and each struggled to gain supremacy over the other in the rise of Christianity in the West. Neither Rome nor the Turks went under in the contest. The bastion of Christianity on the borders of Asia Minor was so ravaged by the crusading armies of the 'Christian' knights of France and Venice, that it eventually succumbed to the combined might of Islam.

But all this still lies in the future; and we must for the time being return to Greece and Macedonia. With the death of Pericles in 429 B.C., the golden age of classical Greece had reached its zenith, and Philip of Macedonia took Athens as his model. Philip, brought up in Thebes by Epaminondas, was passionately interested in Greece and Greek learning. Seventy-four years after the death of Pericles, Philip assumed the title of King of Macedonia, conquered Thrace and Illyria, laid seige to Byzantium in 340 B.C. and finally, in 338, together with his son, the 'Divine Alexander' overthrew Thebes and Athens. Two years later he was assassinated, and was succeeded by Alexander, who had been a pupil of the great Aristotle.

It is a difficult matter, when racing through time as we are doing, to know where to break off and review the course of history. If, however, such a pause is legitimate, then it may most reasonably be made at the reign of Alexander.

Shortly before his rise to power, Xenophon, Thucydides, and Plato had lived and worked in Greece and Asia Minor, and Demosthenes had delivered his famous Philippic orations against Alexander's father. Among the young king's contemporaries, too, there were many eloquent and gifted men: Aristotle of Stagira; Praxiteles, who, with Phidias, was the greatest sculptor of the ancient world; Ephorus of Cuma; Epicurus of Athens; Euclid and Archimedes from the classical school of Alexandria. Alexander, having completed the conquest of Greece and destroyed Thebes, laid his plans for a great campaign against the Persians. He crossed the Hellespont with 25,000 men, defeated the Persians at Granicus and freed the Ionian colonies. Then on he went through Phrygia — clinging to the belief that "strength is the highest of all virtues". It was certainly the major virtue of this Macedonian hero imbued with the culture of Greece. Here was no ordinary man, as Philip, his father, had long since realised, for even as a boy he would stop at nothing. Confronted with the choice of subduing the unruly Thracians and Illyrians, or of extending the power of his Greek-Macedonian kingdom beyond the frontiers of Hellenism, he immediately chose to strike a blow at the mighty Persian Empire.

To-day Greece, Serbia and Bulgaria all claim to have been the cradle of the Macedonian people; but it is difficult to determine the real origins of this bold nation which was — and is — so independent, just, law-abiding and sturdy. Their language is a Slav dialect, and they still preserve their proud, warlike character of the past. Both they and the Montenegrans — though perhaps these people of the 'Black Mountains' are better known to us — are sons of the Balkans, and may have a distant kinship with the Basques, or even with that first primitive tribe which inhabited Asia Minor. Who can guess, and who can ever know? At all events, from this stock came Alexander, later to be known as 'the Great' . . .

At certain times, and with a certain regularity, nature seems to produce great men who embody all the characteristics of their race. To them it is given to bring one period of history to a close, and to lay the foundations of a new era. They leave their mark on the evolution of mankind, and, after a few short years of world-shaking activity, disappear as quickly as they came, into the mists of history. Take Alexander, Julius Caesar and Augustus. During the waning of the Age of Aries these three were preparing the way for a new epoch in men's lives, the Age of Pisces, beginning with the birth of Jesus of Nazareth and reaching its zenith under Constantine the Great. Then Attila and his Huns came to fulfil their task in the scheme of things. European civilisation did not crumble before the invading Germanic hordes, and from the ashes of the old Roman Empire, there rose the structure of the new 'Holy Roman Empire', more powerful than ever under its mighty Christian ruler, Charlemagne, and destined to endure for a thousand years. Such was its strength that it not only halted the invading Magyars at Lechfeld and hurled back the Turks from the very gates of Vienna, but even overcame the turbulent wrath of Islam by the might of the Cross. Napoleon, in his turn, stood at the beginning of the Age of Aquarius, which a figure like Stalin may well have brought to an end. These are all landmarks in the course of history, all placed there by the Almighty. Their rise is meteoric, these empire-builders of Eurasia, and they often burn themselves out before they can realise their great dreams.

But to return to that decisive year, 333 . . .

It was then that Darius II of Persia fled before Alexander, and in 331 B.C. that Alexander, on his victorious march from Gaugamela, captured Susa and Babylon. Two years later he razed the Persian capital, Persepolis, and conceived the dream of a world empire under Macedonian rule. On into India the brilliant young general led his conquering army, so that we find Hellenistic traits permeating Indian philosophy. But the great dream was shattered in 323, when he succumbed to fever at Babylon. His conquests had spread the spirit of Hellenism across the whole of the eastern Mediterranean, and the deeds of the Greek gods were recounted even on the slopes of Mount Lebanon. His attempt to create a common civilisation had provided an important bridge in Asia Minor, over which the future monotheistic faith would eventually pass to Europe.

Alexander's death came as a great blow: but though the Macedonian Empire disintegrated, the small kingdoms which we have already noted continued to exist for centuries, preserving the Hellenistic influence in Asia Minor, while the great city on the Propontis steadily increased her power, maintaining her sovereignty over this ancient world as long as Syria and Anatolia were in her possession. Her influence soon extended beyond even the Balkans or Syria or Asia Minor: she became the stronghold of Greek culture, despite the rivalry of Rome.

We have come to the threshold of the first Christian year (in actual fact 7 B.C.), when Saturn and Jupiter reigned together in the Palestinian heaven.

"And it came to pass in those days, that there went out a decree from Caesar Augustus . . ."

The Romans at that time held Palestine, Syria, Cilicia, Cappadocia, western and northern Asia Minor, Galatia and the whole of Greece and Illyria. Byzantium stood alone, and kept her freedom. The Roman Empire was steadily tightening its hold on the sub-continent. No other world power could hope to break this mighty nation, whose ambition was to possess all Europe, the Near East and North Africa. And yet, one power *did* exist, which would in the end conquer even Rome. True, Christianity was at the outset worsted, and the followers of Jesus scattered and fled before the Roman tyrants. But the more brutal the methods of the Roman pagans grew, the stronger became the faith of the martyred Christians. Immediately after the Crucifixion, the Apostles took refuge in the quiet valley of Antioch, between Mount Lebanon and Anti-Lebanon, where the first great band of followers was formed. We shall speak of this again. Despite the strangle-hold of Rome, then, Christianity spread through Asia Minor, which became the Motherland of the new faith. In A.D. 193 Septimius Severus, having at length captured Constantinople, quelled an uprising in the city. In addition to extending the existing wall, he built temples and aqueducts, one of which still functions to-day. It was Severus who renamed the great port Antonia . . . However, her real golden age only began with the rise of Christianity. By about the year A.D. 100 the Christians had established the first ecclesiastical hierarchy, and after A.D. 200, the religion really started to come to the fore in Anatolia. Meantime Rome's power was shifting more and more towards the East, and it was Constantine the Great who, as early as A.D. 313, gave Christianity official protection by the Edict of Milan, finally proclaiming it the religion of the Roman Empire in 325. Although he himself was a heathen and remained one to his death, he nevertheless opened the

Council of Nicaea, and a year later announced that the new Rome, Nova Roma, was to be the capital of the empire. He moved to the great metropolis on the Golden Horn, to which he eventually gave his name. And Constantinople she remained until our own times . . .

Another of his gifts to the capital was a great new city wall, many miles in length; and between the new wall and the old he built a whole new town, for which he brought priceless treasures from the four corners of his mighty empire. Heavy taxes were levied on Rome, Athens and Alexandria, and costly trappings found their way to Constantinople from the treasure-houses of these cities. Pillars, statues and other valuable works of art were likewise hastily brought from Greece. To-day we can still see what remains of them: the church of Irene and the pillar of snakes in the Hippodrome, said to have been brought to Constantinople from Delphi. At Chryso-polis, near the modern town of Üsküdar, there stood a pillar in which some of the priceless relics of Christendom were concealed, including a fragment of the Cross, a morsel of Christ's bread and a piece of His linen. All his life Constantine did much for Constantinople, and in 337, as he lay on his deathbed, he allowed himself to be baptised. His vision of the Cross became world famous: "In hoc signo vinces!"

In A. D. 340 Constantine's far-flung empire was divided between his sons. Constans reigned in western Rome, while Constantius remained in Constantinople. It looked as though Christianity had triumphed. But all was changed with the accession of the Emperor Julian in 361. A cousin of the Emperor Constantine, Julian 'the Apostate' had, while pursuing his studies, become an ardent disciple of the ancient Hellenistic pagan cults, and had moreover been initiated into the sect worshipping the Sun-god Mithra. In Ephesus he set himself to study the old inscriptions, but in the end he did in fact bring himself to carry on in the Christian faith. His attempts to turn back the wheel of time were doomed to failure, for his temples to Apollo remained empty. Never-theless, in the two short years of his reign the Christian faith was put to a hard test; and when he fell in battle in 363, during a successful campaign against the Persians, it could be said of him also that he had done much for his empire.

The last emperor to rule over both eastern and western Rome was Theodosius the Great (A. D. 379—395). He was responsible for the second, still greater city wall of Constantinople, which remained intact until the Turks captured the city one thousand and six years later. No less than 132 towers now guarded the perimeter of the capital, and the ancient wall still forms the official city boundary of Istanbul. It is probably one of the most typically oriental characteristics of Constantinople that the popery of the Roman emperors could in fact be established within her walls. Just as Sargo saw himself as the representative of his god Marduk, so the eastern Roman emperors set themselves up as God's most powerful vicars on earth.

In the second ecclesiastical council, held at Constantinople, the equal rights of the bishops of that city and of Rome were promulgated. In the wake of advancing Christianity there now lay the ruins of the pagan temples: in 388 Christmas was introduced as a major festival in the Christian calendar; and in 391 all pagan cults were prohibited. Christianity was to be the sole religion of the empire. In Europe the first Germanic colonies were being established in Roman territory, and the pounding of the Huns on the gates of the eternal city was the signal for the hordes of the Visigoths and Ostrogoths to sweep southward into the Italian peninsula.

After the death of Theodosius in A. D. 395 came the final separation between eastern and western Rome. His sons, Honorius and Arcadius, took over the reins of government, the former in the West and the latter in the East, where he ruled until 408. (A stone head of Arcadius was unearthed a few years ago by the Turkish archaeologist Nezih Firath, during alterations to Bayezid Square in Istanbul.)

By 400, therefore, the Christianising of the Roman Empire was complete, and the empire itself divided into two parts. But Byzantium alone withstood the attacks of her enemies for a further thousand years, while the western empire crumbled before the invasions from the north. As early as 425 the University of Constantinople was founded, and the Councils of Ephesus and Chalcedon gave proof of the continuing shift of power to the East and of the growing importance of the Christian Church in eastern Rome. Though Pope Felix excommunicated the Patriarch of Constantinople in 484, thus causing the first schism within the Church, the Emperor Justinian healed this rift in 519, by formally recognising the canons of the Council of Chalcedon.

Justinian reigned from 527 to 565, a period of tremendous growth within the Church. He was the most important of the later eastern Roman emperors, and under him Constantinople's power soared to dazzling heights. During this time Greek ousted Latin as the official language of the empire. The reign of this emperor and his Cypriot consort Theodora was crowned by the construction of the famous Hagia Sophia church, which even to-day must rank as the most imposing Christian church in the world. It took 10,000 workmen barely six years to create this monumental edifice, whose huge interior could easily hold the whole of St Peter's, built a thousand years later. Justinian adorned his church with all manner of treasures culled from his vast domains . . .

By A. D. 537 this wonder of the Christian world was completed, and the Roman Empire stood based on eastern Rome. But the glory of Constantinople aroused the greed of her many enemies. Antioch, fourth city of the empire, was razed by the Persians in 540; in 571 Mahomet was born; the Slavs colonised the Balkans; and in 622 the Avars, Slavs and Persians all laid siege to Constantinople, while the Arabs, too, sought to gain possession of the 'City of Bliss'. In 674—78 and again in 717—18 the Saracens (Arabs) renewed their efforts to snatch the gleaming prize.

Between A. D. 700 and 840 there grew up an eastern Turkish kingdom on the Aral Sea, whose peoples gradually came under the influence of Islam. Turkish runic inscriptions testify to the intellectual development of this nation, which lay outside the limits of present-day Turkey. Ancient documents and other evidence dating from 740 indicate that there was also a western Turkish state which, like the other, had come under the influence of Islam.

In Europe, meantime, the Holy Roman Empire had been founded, and in 812 the Frankish-Byzantine Treaty of Aachen was concluded, by which the Adriatic and Venetian domains were ceded to Constantinople. The Norse sea-rovers, the Varangians, laid siege to the city about this time, but without success. The Russians suffered similar setbacks later.

The plundering tribes of the Magyars threatened the Holy Roman Empire between 934 and 942, at a time when, under Constantine VII (945—63) work was in progress which was to benefit the whole of the western world. Byzantine learning and art had reached hitherto unattained heights, and an Encyclopaedia was compiled which provided a unique source of knowledge for all European scholars in later years, when all the libraries of the West had been destroyed. In Europe the Magyars were beaten off in 955 — those same Magyars who had twice vainly besieged Constantinople before establishing themselves in the Balkans. The Bulgars were overthrown, and remained under eastern Roman suzerainty for two hundred years.

Now the Seljuk Turks, that warlike people of Mesopotamia, came to power, and from 1039 began to subdue great tracts of Persia and Asia Minor. Their prince, Alp Arslan, took Jerusalem in 1070, and went on to conquer Syria and Hedjaz, together with the holy places of Islam, Mecca and Medina. It was to stem this advance and free Jerusalem that the Crusades came into being. From 1096—1099 the armies of the First Crusade fought against the Seljuks in Asia Minor and conquered Palestine, under Geoffroi de Bouillon. The Second Crusade, led by the Hohenstaufen emperor Conrad III, brought only reverses: nor did Barbarossa's ill-fated Third Crusade reach its goal, though it succeeded in forcing its way through the territory of eastern Rome. After his death the armies broke up, having gained a few minor victories; and in 1198 the Order of Teutonic Knights was founded at Acre, the last outpost of the Crusaders on the Syrian coast.

The crusading knights had made the mistake of grossly misjudging the high level of the Persian-Islamic civilisation permeating the Holy Land. However, the power of the Seljuk kingdom in Asia Minor began to wane from the advent of these Christian armies, and an important factor in all this, as we have tried to show previously, was the Cilician border-zone. The Third Crusade advanced no further than Cilicia, while the Fourth Crusade did not even start on its southward march, but spent itself in the capture of Constantinople, which it sacked in true barbarian style! The Doge of Venice, Enrico Dandalo, in conjunction with a group of French knights under Count Baudouin of Flanders, planned to put an end to the schism of 1054 — since when the west-Roman Church had been virtually separated from the Orthodox Church of the East — by punishing Constantinople. Eastern Rome had already lost all her influence in the Balkans: Byzantine suzerainty had been shaken off in Serbia and the Hungarians had conquered Dalmatia. In Asia Minor, too, as well as in Illyria (the Balkans), the eastern empire had suffered setbacks. Venice took every possible advantage of her right of free trade with the whole empire, a right which had been granted in 1082. However, one of the main motives for the formation of this Third Crusade was certainly the still fabulous wealth of Constantinople.

By means of a daring plan proposed by the German Peter Plank, this holy army breached the sea-wall of the city in 1204 and took her by storm. In the course of her history, she had been captured four times — once by Alcibiades, once by Septimius Severus, and again by Constantine; but few people are aware that it was this fourth defeat which undermined the whole structure of the mighty eastern empire. It brought the power of Constantinople so low that when this new 'Latin Empire' finally came to an end, its influence both in Illyria and in Asia Minor had been completely shattered!

22

The great metropolis was overrun and her treasures looted, so that to-day we find them scattered all over Europe as holy relics in Christian churches, her Greek population decimated and her daughters ravished by the lewd, drunken mercenaries. The sacred 667-year-old Hagia Sophia became the scene of the most extravagant orgies. Naked harlots were laid on her altars and black masses celebrated, while the 'Christians' feasted and drank before the communion tables and divine relics of the Greeks, committing every kind of sacrilege in that ancient Christian sanctuary. The church's gold was stolen, her relics and icons 'disappeared' — and all this in the name of Christianity!

Over in Asia Minor, the menace of Islam grew, and a strong and ancient people were preparing to claim the inheritance of the Seljuk nation. At almost the same time, the Mongols found a new and brilliant leader who gathered the tribes of the East about him — Turks, Turkomans, Persians, Seljuks and the rest — and marched against a weakened Europe. This was Genghis Khan, famous, too, among the Turks, who honour him as their own ruler.

In the holy city of Byzantium the rapacious Christians wrought shame upon their brothers of the Faith. Here the power of the decadent West was shattered. The Arabs may well have thought that these unprincipled soldiers had indeed made of the great citadel a "home of bliss" — at least according to Islamic conceptions. And what of the Greeks? Surely they must have felt like Christian martyrs! Was this the Christianity of the West? How different was the honourable struggle of the Third Crusade from that of the Venetians!

Two hundred and fifty years later the forces of Islam at last succeeded in capturing this ravaged city. But how did the Ottoman Turks treat their prize? True to their ancient principle of religious toleration, they spared the faith of the 'Infidels', and Istanbul remains to-day the metropolitan see of Greek Christians. The Sultan admittedly rode his horse into the Church of Hagia Sophia, but forbade any destruction and, kneeling down under the great cupola, gave thanks to Allah: "God is the light of heaven and of the earth." Like every Islamic ruler before him, he guaranteed universal freedom of worship and the liberty of the individual. And that in 1453!

In the fifty-seven years that the Latin Empire of Constantinople survived, irreparable damage was done both to city and empire. But the ascription of their decline to the Turks is a travesty of history. The holy city of Byzantium was destroyed by the armies of Christendom!

In 1261 the Palaeologue emperor, who had fled to Nicaea, recaptured Constantinople. This was the fifth time the port had been taken by force; but soon she would lose all her hinterland. Small forces of Turks had penetrated to the highlands in the interior of Anatolia, where they first of all joined up with their Seljuk kinsmen — whose vassals they were — until their leader, Osman (the name was later corrupted to Ottoman) stormed the town of Brussa (Bursa) in eastern Anatolia and founded the Ottoman Empire in 1288. The Ottomans occupied the territory of the Seljuks and overthrew the weakened, though still highly civilised Seljuk kingdom. From this point we can date the rise of the Turks. In 1291 Acre, the last foothold of the Crusaders, fell to the forces of Islam led by the Ottomans, to be followed in 1341 by Nicaea, at the gates of Constantinople; and in 1354 the conquerors set foot on European soil for the first time at

Gallipoli. They had fully exploited the weakness of the betrayed eastern Roman Empire! As early as 1389 they crippled the Slavs in the fateful battle of Amselfeld, and Kosovop brought home to Europe the extent of the new danger which threatened from the East. The speed with which these events took place is also an indication that the Turks felt confident in by-passing the eastern Roman domains, without fear of attack on their exposed flank.

From 1360, however, another power arose to menace the Ottoman Empire from the rear. The dreaded Mongolian Empire of Genghis Khan had disintegrated after the death of the great king, and only isolated fragments of it remained around the Caucasus, in Iran and in Asia Minor. But now there came a prince of pure Mongolian blood to rouse Asia to fresh conquests: 'lame' Timur — Tamerlane!

When Timur invaded Anatolia, Sultan Bayezid, the Thunderbolt, was besieging Constantinople, whose power now scarcely extended further than its own encircling walls and, across the straits, guarded by chains, to the military encampments on the far shore. The Sultan abandoned the siege, and led his army by forced marches southward to intercept Timur at the Halys. The Ottomans were defeated in the battle of Ankara in 1402, and Bayezid died in captivity. Constantinople had been reprieved! But the power of the Mongols collapsed in its turn, while that of the Ottomans revived, and in 1422 the Golden Horn again saw the Turkish armies coming to the attack. This time they were commanded by the Sultan Murad II, father of the city's future conqueror, Mehemet II. Once more the Turks were forced to relinquish their project, despite their solemn vow to take the great fortress. They turned towards Thrace and the Balkans, and removed their Sultan's capital from Bursa to Adrianople. But they did not relax. All the time they were arming, while Constantinople steadily lost strength, and even paid tributes to the Ottoman Sultans . . .

There is a passage in the Koran where Mahomet prophesies the downfall of Constantinople — a city coveted by the prophet himself — which he orders his followers to bring about. In Islam there were certain orders of monks whose dervishes wielded an enormous spiritual influence on the development of the empire. For these men, such a goal appeared as the sole purpose of life. They were entrusted with the education of the padishahs, and the great Murad already possessed one of these religious preceptors . . .

Murad had set himself the task of fulfilling the prophecy of the Koran. One day, in the presence of his son, Mehemet, of the monk, and of numerous viziers, he spoke of his goal and boasted that he would yet attain it. The monk, however, shook his grey head. "Not you . . . but the boy here will achieve that great purpose," he said, indicating the little five-year-old Mehemet. "And this dervish will support him . . .!" Beside the young heir stood a small, youthful dervish. "Marshallah", whispered the onlookers . . . From that day onward the young dervish suffered bitterly from Murad's jealousy. He was banished from the court and wandered throughout Asia Minor. But when Murad did not achieve his ends, the young Mehemet recalled the monk. They became inseparable friends, and indeed the dervish Ak-Shem-Seddin played a significant rôle in European history, for he was the moving spirit in the capture of Constantinople. Ak-Shem-Seddin — which approximates in Arabic to "White Sun of Religion" — fulfilled the promise of his name.

After prolonged contact with the soldierly Turks, one can no longer regard this last conquest of Constantinople as an individual military feat achieved by the 24-year-old Sultan Mehemet II. Certainly the new Sultan was a military genius, the personification of the whole Turkish warrior-race. His father Murad had set himself to consolidate the strength of the sturdy Turkish army, and a considerable fleet lay ready for the attack. But chains still barred all access to the Golden Horn, and the crescent which had long held sway over Byzantium, and which was no good omen for the Turks, shone refulgent over the kingdom of Constantine XIII.

Though the relieving armies of Rome and Europe were far away, the citizens of Constantinople did not lose hope. To save themselves they would even have been prepared to be absorbed into the Roman Church; but the Balkan Turks and hundreds of miles lay between them and the West! Despite their general military supremacy, and in particular the superiority of their artillery, the Turks engaged in all kinds of intrigue and counter-intrigue with their enemies. Conditions were made and compromises attempted, all of which proves that Mehemet II was unsure of his victory. On hearing that the Roman armies were but twenty-two days from Constantinople, he was on the point of abandoning the struggle, though his ships had been dragged overland on greased rails from the Bosporus to Kazimpasha on the Golden Horn, to avoid the chains guarding the sea-lane. At this juncture an event occurred about which Europe neither knows nor cares! There arose the spiritual genius of Islam. Ak-Shem-Seddin came before his pupil, the Sultan, and counselled him not to lose sight of the goal of Mahomet. Did not Turkish troops still stand between the Roman reinforcements and the 'little Romans' of Byzantium? Still Mehemet hesitated. Supposing the Christians did break through? And now it was Ak-Shem-Seddin's turn to prophesy victory . . . "It is written in the Koran that Islam shall conquer!" . . . He opened the Koran at random . . . "Look here, O Sultan — it is written here on page . . . [I forget which page] . . . that Islam will storm the Christian citadel!" At the young leader's question "When?", he showed him another page . . . "To-day!" "And where?" asked the Sultan — "At this gate!"

At the appointed hour and the appointed place, Mehemet struck, and carried all before him. Byzantium had fallen, the Greek emperor was slain, and the victorious shouts of the Turks rose up to the silver moon, floating like a little white ship above the Golden Horn. Then Eyoup, the swordbearer of the Prophet, who long ages before had fallen at these same walls, was hailed as the hero of the Turks, the true victor of Constantinople, and he swept like a sword of Islam over the unhappy Greeks . . .

How many Europeans know this side of the story? So fell the eastern empire of Orthodox Christianity. Its final defeat was not due entirely to the carefully planned and well-supported strategy of the Ottomans. Behind their more fully developed military skill stood something else; it was the strong and aggressive spirit of Islam, embodied in the sage Ak-Shem-Seddin!

The faith which moved the Turks at Constantinople is still as powerful; and present-day Turks believe as firmly as ever in the greatness of Allah and of His Prophet . . . It is this faith which constitutes the most unshakable barrier against the godlessness of Bolshevism.

In the night following the battle, the victorious young general, thereafter known as 'Fatih' — the conqueror — was torn by a deep inner conflict. It is historically true that he sought out his teacher in the old man's tent, threw himself at his feet and humbly begged to be received into the order of dervishes to which Ak-Shem-Seddin belonged, now that he had fulfilled the task laid down in the Koran . . . The aged monk raised his young master up, and, as the horns were heralding a new day and a new era in the history of the city, he told his lord and Sultan: "Your task, O Lord, is just beginning! Do you not hear the call of your brave warriors? My task is done, and it is for me to return to the wide lands of Anatolia and the confines of my monastery!" With these words, Ak-Shem-Seddin, the "White Sun of Mahomet", left the tent and made his way back across the Bosporus . . . an unknown dervish who had accomplished his mission in the spirit of the faith . . .

This is the Turkish view of the fall of Constantinople, and we do well to realise that this victory was of a very different nature from that of the Venetians and French, those 'soldiers of Christ'. And now the way to Vienna lay open! But history shows that it was not given even to the mighty forces of Islam to expand with impunity beyond the territories around the Bosporus, and four hundred and fifty years later the Ottomans, too, shared the fate of so many of the peoples of Asia Minor . . . Now, however, the rest of the eastern Roman domains quickly fell to the Turks. In 1461 the last remnants of Greek resistance were wiped out a Trebizond. The Greek scholars fled first from Constantinople, and then further west from Athens to Italy, as the whole of the Balkans were absorbed by the empire of the Porte. As time went on even the great empire of the Habsburgs was threatened.

This conquest of Constantinople took place at the time when Gutenberg of Mainz was establishing his first printing press, in 1450: Leonardo da Vinci was born in 1452, and Albrecht Dürer in 1471: and a little later, intrepid European adventurers sailed on a great voyage of discovery towards the New World. From 1526 until 1792 the Turks waged threatening wars against the Habsburg empire, and their repeated invasions were as much of a menace to the German people as were the recurrent outbreaks of the dreaded plague! Ten years before the great siege of Vienna, the Portuguese Magellan sailed round the world, and on his return in 1591, Vienna had just withstood the first Turkish onslaught. Ottoman supremacy in Hungary had been recognised since 1562, and more than a century later, when Germany lay exhausted after the Thirty Years' War, when Crete and Podolia had been conquered by the Turks and the plague had carried off thousands of the citizens of Vienna, there came the second, and this time almost fatal siege of that great city.

Her almost miraculous delivery was brought about by the victory of Kahlenberg. The power of the Turks was further weakened and finally crippled in the battles of Zenta in 1697 and Belgrade in 1717. But the Balkans continued to lie for centuries under the yoke of Islam.

The extent of the danger to the West can be judged from the following extract taken from a Turkish pamphlet dated 1683:

> We, by the Grace of God Mola Mohammed, Glorious and All-powerful Emperor of Babylon
> and Judea and of East and West, King of all Earthly and Heavenly Kings, Great King of

Holy Arabia and Mauretania, Hereditary and Renowned King of Jerusalem, Commander and Lord of the Grave of the Crucified God of the Infidels, do pledge our most sacred word to you, the Emperor of Rome and you, the King of Poland, and likewise to all your Allies, that we are about to make war upon your petty kingdoms, and come with 13 Kings and 1,300,000 Infantry and Cavalry, to trample your Lands without Pity or Mercy beneath our horses' hooves; and with this Army, whose Strength neither you nor your Allies can conceive, we shall put you to the Fire and the Sword . . .

But the frontiers at the Bosporus are not so easily crossed — a fact also recognised by the Allies at the end of the first world war, when they were ousted from the eternal city of Byzantium by Kemal Atatürk, and finally lost their international concessions.

In 1923 there began a new era, a new name and a new order in Constantinople. The first year in the reformed Turkish calendar became a symbol for the young Turks. Constantinople was re-born as Istanbul, and all the old decay was swept away to make room for the republican methods of freedom. 'Byzantinism' was confined exclusively to everything which was non-Turkish, Ankara was made the capital, and the modern Turkish state was infused with fresh vigour and initiative. Turkey turned towards Europe with revolutionary ardour. Atatürk took it for granted that every Turk was naturally a Muslim: but he abolished the all-powerful Caliphate with its semi-divine Sultans: he forbade the wearing of the 'Greek' fez and the veil: he drew up modern laws on the western pattern, so that Turkey could take her place alongside the occidental states. All these things, and more, were accomplished by him in the setting up of the new Turkey, which, though now confined to Asia Minor, was nevertheless strong and flourishing. And there Allah still rules to-day; he is the all-powerful and the only God. Let us not forget this as we tread this land of a thousand gods — and the One!

The Ineffable remains a mystery to us, who cannot comprehend the language of Allah. This quiet, almost exclusive speech of Islam and the strange spirit of the East stop short to-day, as always, at the fast-flowing waters of the Bosporus. And indeed this is as it should be. Here Cross and Crescent have established their frontiers, and here, too, the hammer and sickle would come to grief on the strong defences created by Atatürk under the banner of the white crescent on its red field, symbol of the new Turkish nation.

A Thousand Gods — and One God

It would be beyond the scope of this volume of photographs to enumerate fully the myriad gods of Asia Minor, the protecting and fortune-bringing deities of so many ancient tribes . . . or to classify their relationships to the Indo-Germanic gods or their connections with similar or kindred, though differently-named figures. We are only concerned with their flowering in the soil of Anatolia, the conception of their mythological origins and their diffusion in all directions — but more especially westwards to Greece and thence into the sphere of our own culture.

Astronomically speaking, a solar month has a duration of two thousand years, a fact probably known to these ancient Mesopotamian civilisations for centuries, since at that time the knowledge of astronomy and astrology was more widespread than in the world of to-day. This unit of measurement is a considerable help when it comes to dealing with prehistoric times. Every two thousand years or so, the sun passes through one of the signs of the zodiac. It was in Taurus from the fourth to the second millennium B.C., and it was surely no mere coincidence that during that time the bull was an object of worship, just as it was not simply a matter of chance that in the succeeding Ages of Aries and Pisces — the former lasting from the second millennium B.C. until the Birth of Christ and the latter from then until A.D. 2000 — the ram, Pan and the ancient Christian symbol of the fish were likewise treated with reverence. The discovery of the planet Uranus by Herschel fell at the beginning of the Age of Aquarius, whose sign was already used by scientists to denote direct current, motive power and infinity. In these vast tracts of time, the transition periods of three to six hundred years are confused, and point to the disappearance of the existing order in preparation for the unknown developments yet to come. It is clear that we are going through just such a transitional phase at present.

At the time when the bull was worshipped, the gods were still represented as robust and powerful. Just as man had to defend himself heroically against the unfathomable cruelty of Nature, so did his deities. It was on the shores of Asia Minor that Zeus came down in the form of a bull and, taking the lovely Europa on his back, carried her off to the West. To this age also belong the dance round the golden calf and the adoration of the sacred bull Apis in Egypt. The he-goat of the cult of Dionysus, Pan, also found as a stag or even an antelope, dominates the Age of Aries until the rise of Christianity. Since Christ's Apostles were fishermen, the first secret symbol of the new faith was the fish, and fish is still the food of fast-days. But whence came the gods? From which conception does the idea of a unique God emanate?

The disappointment of human hopes is at the root of the creation of gods — and the recognition of an all-creating, supernatural force governing human existence leads to God. It is a far cry from the naïve concepts of the early bull-worshippers to the spiritual maturity of the Age of Aquarius, when men pressed forward to the frontiers of Nature, there to sense the presence of God . . .

Even the specialist finds it difficult to differentiate between imported and native gods. The original inhabitants of Asia Minor had different deities from those of the incoming Hittites of Indo-Germanic stock. The favourite god of the warlike Hittite hunters was the stag-god Rundas. In their new country they came upon the unfamiliar winged Ishtar, weather-god of the Protohatti, whom they adopted as a second god. If Rundas recalls the delicacy of St. Hubert's stag, Ishtar is much more oriental, a little like the idols of Indonesia. Even though the European origin of the Hittite Rundas was forgotten, he still remained, reigning side by side with the Great Mother Kupapa. There is a whole galaxy of these figures, who rise before us like a great army as we traverse the sacred region of Yazilikaya.

The stag standards, exquisite examples of the smith's craft, dating back to the third millennium B.C., which were discovered in the tombs of Alaja Höyük, were symbols of good fortune, carried into battle and to the hunt, and were also used in religious ceremonies to represant the presence of the beloved god. The development of this stag from the mightier bull can be unmistakably traced, and helps us to recognise more easily the transition from the Age of Taurus to the Age of Aries. Kupapa, the stag's divine consort, seems to appear in the Gilgamesh epic, where there is a monster Humbaba, and we can even trace her in Selencid Syria, where she appears as Kombabos. In the course of the centuries the goddess finally becomes transformed into Cybele, who was adopted by the Romans and later worshipped for a time by Julian the Apostate.

The sturdy Hittites were a ceremonious and fair-minded people. Not only did they take every opportunity to do honour to their own gods which they had brought with them, but they saw to it that no strange god should be offended, and that the special deities of every city in their domains should be treated with respect. And so we find a great variety of names attributed to the same god. It was a matter of no great importance. The weather-god was Tarhund; but he was also Teshup or Taru, and in Syrian Adad or Namman. This same weather-god was apparently taken over from ancient Anatolian tribes who had inhabited the region. Tarhund became Tarkondemus, and is akin to the Etruscan Tarchon. So, too, the Roman Tarquins can trace their name back to the original form.

The Hittites had a patriarchal form of society, in which everything revolved round the king, who, on his death, would himself in all probability become a god. Likewise their whole gathering of gods forms a great family, with Kupapa at the centre, the Great Mother, Sun Goddess of Arinna.

> Sun Goddess of Arinna, my mistress, queen of all the earth,
> In the land of Hatti thou art called Sun Goddess of Arinna,
> But in that land where thou hast caused thy cedars to flourish,
> There thou art called Hepat . . .

So runs an old Hittite text . . . In the family of Arinna we come across a host of relations, grandsons and grand-daughters of the weather-gods, like Zintuhi, one of the grand-daughters, or Telipinu, god of childhood, known in Cilicia as Sarma, with his mother Hepatsarma. This Telipinu is the mischief-maker among the gods, and his pranks cause tremendous confusion in Nature. Thunder and lightning add to the tumult, until all is restored to order and Telipinu is safely ensconced on his mother's knee. He is the god of all growing things, and eventually becomes the adult Dionysus of the Greeks, whose licentious behaviour points to his Anatolian background. The god of childhood has become the wine-god of Olympus.

The god of harvests, deities connected with Ishtar, mountain and river gods, gods of streams, winds and clouds, protecting and wrathful gods and even gods whose special duty is to defend wanderers — all these and more are found in the different civilisations of this region. They spread from the hills down across the plains to the sea, and some, like Cybele and Dionysus, penetrated even further into the culture of the West. The cremation of dead heroes, and the subsequent burial of their ashes, remind us of similar ceremonies in the epics of Homer, while the giant Hahhimas, who imprisons the gods at the onset of winter, surely has his counterpart in the Nordic sagas. And finally, there is a nameless god who rules over the fate of mankind — 'my god' — Siunasmis.

But the central figure in the hieroglyphs on the cliffs of Yazilikaya is always Kupapa-Sausga, together with Rundas. This Kupapa, with her flowing robes and weapons of war, attended by two handmaidens, becomes the Greek Nike, goddess of victory, while Asia Minor's Tyche looks very like Cybele.

The Hittites adopted many of the Babylonian interpretations of dreams, as well as their prophecies; and the consulting of oracles provided the third and most direct means of ascertaining the inclinations of the gods. And always their Indo-Germanic thoroughness caused them to avoid insulting or neglecting even one of these many divinities . . .

Warm beer was the staple drink of the people, and they also had honey, milk and wine. Enormous earthenware vessels were used to store their supplies; and they drank from silver tankards very like those we know today. The finely-wrought golden crowns of their rulers and their wonderful ceramics, point to a very high level of culture. In their homes they had furniture, dishes for keeping food hot, and seats and cushions as well as beds and corn-mills. Their weapons were of copper and bronze; but their religious vessels were wrought of iron, lead, silver and gold. For trading, their currency was silver ingots, and they loved all kinds of games and sports — especially chariot racing, as we have seen. From them — or at least from this land — the Habsburgs borrowed their symbols of the two-headed eagle and the golden fleece.

They were truly a great and ancient people. The Old Testament numbers them among the oldest tribes of Syria at the time of Abraham, and when Europe's first town-dwelling civilisation was started in Crete about 1600 B.C., Hattusa was already almost four hundred years old!

The Great Mother of the gods, reigning in Asia Minor as Kupapa and in Rome as Cybele, also appears as Diana of Ephesus and serves as a model for Demeter. Is it, then, so astonishing that the Great Mother of Christianity was born and died in this land? It is a long road from Ephesus to Bethlehem and back . . .

The advent of Christ shook the unsophisticated polytheistic ideas of the Age of Aries to their foundations, and brought to mankind a new concept of the universal love of a single, eternal and all-powerful deity. The simple fishermen of Galilee found it difficult to understand the majesty of a God of Love, and to carry on His teaching after His death. It was understandable that that small band of Christians should flee from the Romans to a place of safety, if they were to bear witness to their faith. And when, faced with the conviction of the apostles of monotheism, the anxiety of the Romans grew until they eventually took measures to suppress the Christians, these faithful followers of the Cross fled by way of Antioch and Tarsus to the city of Ephesus.

Between A.D. 40 and 50 there was formed in the town of Antioch in the shadow of Mount Lebanon the first Christian community under the leadership of the Apostle Peter. Here, too, they were first given the name "Christiani" and from here they took their separate ways, armed with their faith, to spread the gospel of love, equality and brotherhood throughout the Roman Empire. The first church still stands at the Turkish Antakya (Antioch) in Hatay, and is administered by four Christian bishops, though none of them is actually resident. The caves can still be seen where the Christians concealed themselves in order to carry on their great work, and one can tread the very spot where the youthful Peter pledged himself to Christ. But this historic place has suffered shameful neglect. Beyond the limits of the present-day town, which is built over the ruins of Syria's most ancient city — stands the simple church in the rocks. Mosaics cover its floor; but they are broken and crumbling now, and unscrupulous traders sell as 'mementoes' pieces of them which are found scattered over a wide surrounding area. "The old order changeth . . ."

It is the same in Tarsus. There one may still see part of the antique west gate, through which Paul may have passed; but nothing more recalls the golden age of the Tarsus of two thousand years ago. In Cappadocia, on the contrary, traces of the fugitive Christians are still numerous. It is not only the ancient cave-churches, the communion tables and the famous frescoes, but the whole atmosphere of this deserted city of the monks which gives the impression of mystic unreality.

The eroded countryside was doubtless occupied at one time by the Hittites, for the simple, flat-roofed mud dwellings of the villages are very reminiscent of Hittite architecture. To-day, broad highways lead the traveller from Kayseri (formerly Caesarea) past the 13,000-feet-high Mount Erciyas into this lonely valley with its melodious place-names. Fantastic rock-formations stand guard over age-old vineyards which were once tended by the monks, and one could almost believe oneself transported back over the centuries to a happier era. The lively Cappadocian children peep out at us from the spy-holes of the monks' cells fifty feet above, apparently quite at home in these old caves.

The holy men must have found this an ideal place both for prayer and for the cultivation of the vine . . . the hot sun beats fiercely down . . . and the fruits of the valley are of a rare and wonderful sweetness . . .

And here a scene from the Bible seems to focus before our eyes. A truly apostolic face looks out with majestic composure across the distant vineyards of this fertile valley, while nearby a donkey plods round and round in an endless circle, pushing the heavy stone that grinds the corn; and mothers with their children fill their jars with cool, pure water from the ancient Hittite springs . . . It was indeed a glorious dream, that vision of Paul and the first Christian monks . . .

Thousands of miles lie between this lovely valley and the west coast of Anatolia. The cedars still grow on the slopes of the high hills, and there, at 4,600 feet, lives the dromedary of the desert, which seems to thrive and which certainly fits into the southern landscape. Here, too, we find bears, and little Anatolian donkeys drag along slaughtered wild pigs of enormous size. Vultures and eagles circle — as they do even over Ankara — high above some forgotten carcase. Valuable Turkish carpets are woven by many-pigtailed little girls sitting by the wayside, and the steep roads skirt the coast high above the white-crested waves of the Mediterranean. All the time the sun beats pitilessly down . . . but cool, limpid streams flow down from the hills into the White Sea. Then, Antalya — city of a thousand such streams; we pass on, the road leading once more into the mountains. Still more beautiful and more valuable carpets are made here, and magnesium lakes line the route into the valley of Smyrna, renowned for its figs. We are approaching the biblical Laodicea and the cascading chalk-cliffs of Hierapolis, which the Turks call 'Pamukkale' —

the 'cotton-wool castle'. Here broken Greek pillars are reflected in the blue waters of the hot springs. The road goes on, to Sardis and finally to Selejki.

A Seljuk fortress dominates the once-famous valley, and all is quiet in this Turkish village with its foreign traffic. Below the fortress once lay the golden temple of Diana, the wonder of Ephesus, at the spot where we find to-day a quiet pool haunted by the hot rays of the Anatolian sun . . . and if we follow the camels as they disappear behind the olive grove yonder, we come at last to Ephesus. It was here that Homer lived, and saw, rising from the waters of the Cayster, the swans which he afterwards depicted in the Iliad. It was here that the great wave from Palestine broke; here St. Luke, in the historic amphitheatre, admonished and incensed the merchants of the Agora. Here in the Temple of Serapis, Julian the Apostate was received into the mysterious cult of Mithras. Here John baptised the handful of those who had grown tired of Diana and the other pagan gods. Here stood the library of Celsus, and here the Austrian archaeologists uncovered the Temple of Hestia Boulaia with their modern machinery . . .

The cave of the Seven Sleepers is cool and quiet . . . over there stand the ruins of Paul's prison . . . It is a world full of awe and wonder . . .

Six hundred and sixty feet above the remains of the ancient metropolis, beyond the city walls of Ephesus, towers the holy mountain of Meryemanè — the Mother of God. The ascent on foot in the sweltering heat of August is like a road to Golgotha; only 'cattle and Germans' would go out in such heat, said my Turks. The clustering fig-trees are laden with ripe fruit . . . But the climb seems endless. And then the pilgrim raises his tired eyes, and sees before him the simple house of Mary. Streams gush forth from under the holy shrine, while visitors marvel silently in the shadow of giant elms and plane-trees, as old as time itself. Far in the distance stretch the foam-flecked waves of the sea.

This is the most peaceful spot in all Asia Minor. He who follows the steps of that anguished Mother down into the little valley, and listens, will hear the stones whispering of the only true God, omnipotent and ineffable until the end of the world.

The vale of tears in which we live is forgotten in this celestial valley on the Hill of St. Mary at Ephesus, above the White Sea and under the bare, red-gold mountains of Asia Minor.

Great Mother of Arinna . . . Mother Asia Minor . . . Mother Mary. Was it indeed here that the first man, Adam, dreamed his dreams? There lies Corycus, the everlasting Paradise. And between Sun and Crescent stands the eternal Cross . . . From the golden sands of the Cayster all three send forth their light . . . Sun, Cross and Crescent . . .

Maxim Osward

THE HITTITE EMPIRE

1 STATE TEMPLE IN YAZILIKAYA

"The Inscribed Cliffs". Ritual rock carvings in relief in the neighbourhood of the

Hittite Capital of Hattusas (earlier than the third millennium B.C.).

32

2 HITTITE STEER

During the sun cycle of Taurus the Hittites migrated into Asia Minor.   Hittite Museum, Ankara.

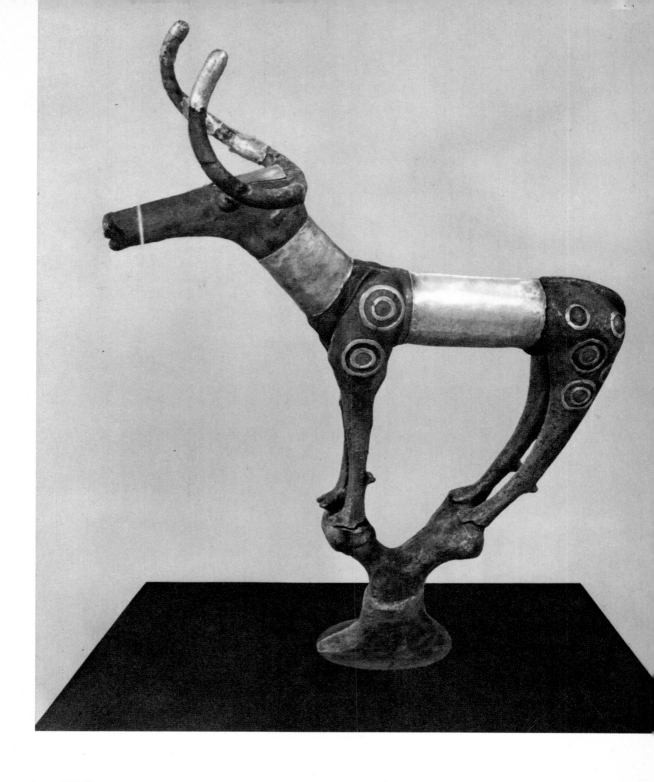

3 BRONZE STAG FROM THE ALAJA HÖYÜK

Figure for a standard ornamented with secret signs in silver (about the third millennium B.C.).

5 RITUAL OBJECT OF THE PRIEST-KINGS

   The stag-god Rundas with a halo and base of copper. Alaja Höyük (third millennium B.C.).

4 RUNDAS, THE HITTITE GOD OF THE CHASE

   Prototype of our stag of St. Hubert; for a standard. Copper object from the

   Royal Tombs of Alaja Höyük (2550—2350 B.C.).

6 HITTITE ARCHERS

Their presence in the state temple during the procession of the gods was essential.

7 HITTITE STONE LIONS

Kayseri Museum (second millennium B.C.).

8 KUPAPA, THE "GREAT MOTHER", "SUN QUEEN OF ARINNA"

Principal Goddess of the Hittites, foreshadowing the Cybele of Asia Minor.

9 DETAIL FROM THE ROCK TEMPLE IN YAZILIKAYA

Procession before the gods.

10 SPHYNX GATEWAY IN ALAJA HÖYÜK

Clearly distinguishable is the double-headed eagle, which we encounter later as symbol

of the Austro-Hungarian monarchy and the Tsarist empire.

11 Maid Servants or Priestesses of the God-Kings

in a ritual procession. From Carchemish. Hittite Museum, Ankara.

12 HITTITE JAR OF PAINTED CLAY

from the Royal Tombs of Alaja Höyük (middle of the third millennium B.C.).

Hittite Museum, Ankara.

13 REPRESENTATION OF HURRIAN WARRIORS

Painted stone. The Hurrians, like the Etruscans, are believed to have been related

to the Hittites. Hittite Museum, Ankara.

14 SILVER JUG FROM THE ROYAL TREASURE OF ALAJA HÖYÜK
A unique gem of Hittite art from the third
millennium B.C. Hittite Museum, Ankara.

15 CLAY JUG FROM THE HITTITE MUSEUM
These handsome Hittites vessels are more than
4000 years old.

16 GOLDEN CROWN OF A HITTITE QUEEN
One of the many valuable finds from the Royal Tombs
of Alaja Höyük (2550—2350 B.C.).

THE PHRYGIANS

17 CARVED LYDIAN TOMBSTONES *About 500 B.C. Museum in Izmir (Smyrna).*

18 SMALL SCULPTURE FROM SMYRNA
*The conquerors of the Hittites, the Phrygians were in their turn subjected to the Greek
cultural influence of Western Anatolia.   About 2,500 years old.*

PLATE 1 BYZANTINE MOSAIC
*Detail of hunting-scene from the road leading from the imperial palace to the Sea of Marmara,
first uncovered by the English. Between 2,300 and 1,700 years old Mosaic-Museum, Istanbul.*

20 DETAIL OF THE SO-CALLED SARCOPHAGUS OF ALEXANDER

Archaeological Museum, Istanbul.

19 ALEXANDER THE GREAT

Stone sculpture from the third century B.C. Found at Pergamum.

Archaeological Museum, Istanbul.

21/22 HARBOUR OF ISKENDERUN (ALEXANDRETTA)
Founded by Alexander the Great's
famous general, Seleucus Nicator.

23 ROMAN DWELLINGS HEWN IN THE ROCK NEAR SAMANDAĞ

between Lebanon and Anti-Lebanon, south of Iskenderun. A health resort for Roman officers.

24 GIANT TUNNEL FOR THE OFFICERS' RESORT NEAR SAMANDAĞ

the ancient port of Antioch, built by the Roman emperor Vespasian.

25 FORE-PART OF ST. PETER'S CHURCH IN ANTAKYA (ANTIOCH)

Here the Apostles gathered together the first community and dwelt like fugitives in the caves.

26 THE FIRST CHURCH OF ST. PETER

In Antioch the Christians were first named 'Christiani'. From here they set out against the Roman world.

28 WOMEN AND GIRLS FROM ANTAKYA (ANTIOCH)
The features of the Macedonian-Greek immigrants are still clearly in evidence in these classical profiles.

27 ON A FARMSTEAD IN ANTAKYA (ANTIOCH)
As it did 2,000 years ago, the indispensable donkey still serves man today.

29 Roman Bridge near Issus

This was the scene of Alexander's bitter battle against the Persians in 333 B.C.

Arrian describes how 'between the armes flaved the stream of Pineros'.

30 THE SHORE AT SAMANDAĞ, LOOKING TOWARDS LEBANON

There lies the Promised Land . . .

31 THE CEREMONIAL "VIA ARCADIA" IN EPHESUS
    The Roman column bears a cross of protest
    against the heathen gods.

32 THE GREAT THEATRE OF EPHESUS
    Built by Claudius A.D. 34—41. At this spot
    St. Luke preached to tens of thousands
    against the cult of Diana.

33 THE CHURCH OF ST. JOHN, ABOVE THE APOSTLE'S GRAVE

In the background, above present-day Selçok, stands the fortress of Ayasluk.

34 VIEW OF THE ANCIENT AGORA IN EPHESUS

The market-place of the ancient town with its many memorials.

35 THE SERAPIS TEMPLE IN EPHESUS

One of the large caryatids of the temple that have been preserved.

36 FLUTINGS OF THE HEAVY TEMPLE GATES

Here the Christian Emperor Julian, later the Roman Emperor Julian the Apostate,

was initiated into the mysteries of the Mithraic cult.

37 REMAINS OF THE GREAT TEMPLE OF DIANA OF EPHESUS

The Pilgrims to this sanctuary, which was one of the 'Seven Wonders', numbered hundreds of thousands.

Herostratus set fire to it in 356 B.C.

The dimensions of the baptismal font — now overrun with weeds — are enormous.

In the year 135 B.C., Celsus Polemaenus of Sardes, Roman senator, was Governor

of the province of Asia. The Library was erected in his honour.

40 PORTION OF THE EAST GYMNASIUM — 'GYMNASIUM OF THE MAIDENS'

Built in the second century B.C.

41 MARBLE CEREMONIAL HIGHWAY

between the Magnesian Gate and the North Gate, endowed by Eutropius,

built in the fourth century A.D.

42 MEMORIAL STONE ON THE MARBLE HIGHWAY IN EPHESUS

43 Pedestal Base from the Church of St. John in Ephesus

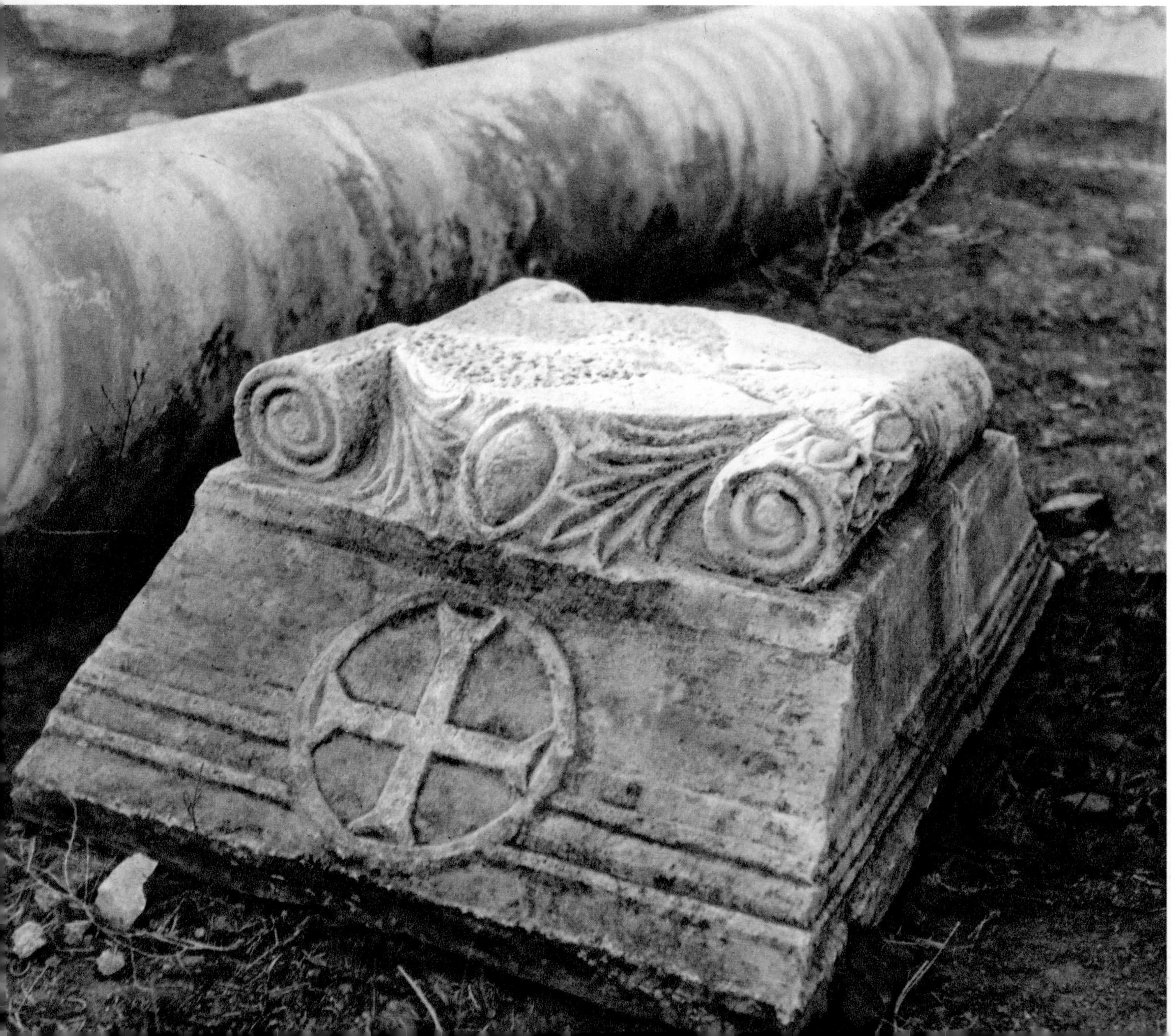

44 MARBLE STONE IN HONOUR OF THE EMPEROR AUGUSTUS ON THE AGORA,

put up by his son-in-law Agrippa and his daughter Julia (during Christ's life-time).

45 PORTION OF THE GROTTO OF THE SEVEN SLEEPERS NORTH-EAST OF MOUNT PION

According to tradition, the Christians laid out their Campo Santo

around the tomb of Mary Magdalene.

46 THE SO-CALLED TOMB OF ST. LUKE

Circular building in the vicinity of the East Gymnasium. The stone slab at the South Gate

shows as symbols the Cross and the Bull.

48 CHURCH OF ST. JOHN AND THE APOSTLE'S TOMB

St. John, to whom Jesus entrusted his Mother, preached here.

His tomb is to this day a well-known place of pilgrimage.

47 COLUMN OF THE CHURCH OF ST. JOHN IN EPHESUS

The Emperor Justinian, who also erected the Hagia Sophia in Constantinople,

had the 'Basilica of St. John' replaced by a magnificent edifice.

The large cross on the column is Byzantine.

49 PANAYA KAPULU, BY THE HILL OF OUR LADY, THE ALADAĞ HILL

The traditional place of birth, residence and death of the Mother of Jesus.

The Lazarites have restored the place with the original stones.

PLATE II INTERIOR OF THE CHAPEL OF OUR LADY ABOVE SELÇUK (EPHESUS)

This chapel, re-erected upon the old foundations, now serves as a place of worship for all religions.

50 ROMAN WINE-JAR AT SELÇUK

Countless Greek and Roman objects
bearing testimony to the past
are to be found in the open and in
the houses; they are still in use.

52 CEILING MOSAIC IN THE KARIYEH CAMI

The old monastery church of Chora dates from the 'Eastern Roman' period of Constantinople.

Today it is the most prized mosque in Istanbul on account of its famous mosaics.

51 TEMPLE OF AUGUSTUS IN ANCYRA

According to tradition, the ancient Ankara was founded by the great Phrygian king,

Midas, in the eighth century B.C.

53 ARCADIUS THE FIRST
'EAST ROMAN' EMPEROR
OF BYZANTIUM
This head was excavated
in the Tauri Forum of
'Eastern Rome' in 1949.
Archaeological Museum,

54 MOSAIC OF A GREEK YOUTH

The Byzantines were the greatest masters of this art. The lustre of the colours has endured for more than a millennium.

55 Byzantine Mosaic

Battle between eagle and snake. Portion of the 40-feet-wide ceremonial road leading from the Byzantine emperor's palace to the Propontis.

56 Hunting scene in the Ceremonial Road

British archaeologists unearthed this mosaic and roofed it over. The site of this find today surrounds the Istanbul Mosaic-Museum.

57   Detail from the Ceremonial Road.   *From the Istanbul Mosaic-Museum; boy playing with hoops.*

58   Remains of the first Hagia Sophia

    The Megale Ekklesia begun by Constantine the Great was consecrated on May 12th, 360.

59 The third Hagia Sophia

The work of the master-builders Anthemius of Tralles and Isidor of Miletus under the guidance

of the Byzantine Emperor Justinian, it was built in the record time of six years by 10,000 workers.

60 South Gallery showing the mosaic-adorned North Front

62–63 MOSAICS IN THE SOUTH GALLERY OF THE HAGIA

a) *Emperor John II Comnenus and his Hungarian consort Eirene. (Twelfth century A.D.)*

b) *The Virgin Mary, Christ and St. John. (Eleventh century A.D.)*

61 SOUTH WING NEXT TO THE DOMED HALL

The walls are covered with a variety of the choicest marbles in many colours, the mighty arches adorned

with priceless gold-mosaics and every marble capital differently carved.

64 MOSAIC IN THE NARTHEX ABOVE THE EMPEROR'S GATE

Christ the Pantocrator with a Basileus — probably the Byzantine Emperor Basil (867—886 A.D.) —
kneeling before him begging forgiveness.

65 THE ANTI-NARTHEX OF THE HAGIA SOPHIA

South entrance with mosaic representing the Virgin Mary and the builders of the 'Holy Wisdom':
left, the Emperor Justinian; right, the Emperor Constantine the Great (about A.D. 1,000).

PLATE III INTERIOR OF THE HAGIA SOPHIA

The elaborate consecration of the Hagia Sophia took place on December 27th, 537,
during the reign of the Emperor Justinian. The large marble vessel for oil (right)
derives from Pergamum and is said to have contained the holy anointing oil.

67 THE KURŞUNLU CAMI IN KAYSERI (CAESAREA)

Prototype of the small-town mosque by Sinan from the sixteenth century known as the 'Leaden Mosque'.

66 MARBLE STATUE OF THE TURKISH MASTER-BUILDER SINAN

in front of Ankara University. Sinan came from Kayseri, created the Turkish type of mosque

and was responsible for the majestic Suleymaniyeh in Istanbul.

69 THE CITY WALL OF KAYSERI (CAESAREA) WITH THE 13,000-FEET-HIGH ERCIYAŞ

This wall was built in the dim past, was frequently restored, was taken by the Osmanli Sultan
Beyazid Yilderim and strengthened by the conqueror of Istanbul, Sultan Mehemet Fatih.

68 DÖNER KÜMBED, THE 'TURNING MAUSOLEUM'

Tomb of a Seljuk Sultana. Kayseri is the city of mausoleums.

70 Hittite Insignia of Rank from the Museum in Kayseri

Royal cartouche from the second millennium B.C.

71 Hittite Hieroglyphic Tablet

Kayseri Museum.

CAPPADOCIA

72–73 THE 43-MILE-LONG GÖREME VALLEY IN CAPPADOCIA

A lunar landscape, already inhabited by the Hittites. West of Kayseri (Caesarea).

74 A ROCK-CHURCH NEAR GÖREME

St. Paul fled hither with other Christians from his Roman persecutors,

and a monastic centre, with convents, monasteries and churches grew up.

75 BETWEEN ÜRKÜB-NEVŞEHIR-AVANOS IN CAPPADOCIA

On the road to Nevşehir through the 'Valley of a Thousand Monasteries'.

76 Rock Fortresses of Tufa

The Christian monks dwelt in this valley and grew their vines.

The Turks now still tend these vineyards.

77 THE GÖREME VALLEY OF REFUGE

Thousands of such rock-caves give the landscape its unique character.

79 WATER IS LIFE — WATER IS PRECIOUS

78 ÜRKÜB IN CAPPADOCIA. *Old Turkish peasant — he recalls the early Christian recluses.*

81   Tomb of Mehemet I in the 'Green Mausoleum'

Built in 1419 by Haci Ayvas on the orders of Sultan Mehemet I (1413—1421).

80   Yeşil Türbe — the 'Green Mausoleum'

in Bursa-Brussa, the first capital of the Osmanli.   THE OSMANLI EMPIRE

83 ARNAVUTKÖY ON THE BOSPORUS

A fishing-village near Istanbul.

82 THE FAMOUS SULEYMANIYEH MOSQUE

On the Golden Horn (Halys) in Istanbul, built by Sinan on the orders
of Suleiman the Magnificent (1550—1557).

84–85 THE BYZANTIUM OF TODAY: GENERAL VIEW OF THE CITY OF ISTANBUL

Travellers compare the city's situation with that of Rio de Janeiro.

86 SULTAN AHMET CAMI – KNOWN AS THE 'BLUE MOSQUE'

Built by Sultan Ahmet I between 1609 and 1617.

87 THE INTERIOR OF THE 'BLUE MOSQUE'

With its faience work and six minarets it is the most beautiful and elegant mosque in Turkey.

89 A DIOGENES OF THE TWENTIETH CENTURY

   This old cobbler of Istanbul lives in a barrel as did Diogenes,

   who was born in this region in the fourth century.

88 THE HIPPODROME OF BYZANTIUM

   Begun by Septimius Severus and finished under Constantine, it was one of the loveliest

   places on earth. Obelisks, serpent pillars, the Hagia and the 'Blue Mosque' still remind one of this.

PLATE IV SCENE IN KADIKÖY

   Kadiköy is the name of the ancient Chalcedon, where in 451 the fourth General Council

   against the Monophysites met. Today it is a part of Istanbul, on the Asian side.

90 THE HILTON HOTEL

On the European Pera Side of present-day Istanbul

stands its most modern hotel.

91 VIEW OF THE NEW CITY QUARTER OF ISTANBUL

from the roof of the great Hilton building.

92 THE ANCIENT CITY WALL OF CONSTANTINOPLE

In 1453 the Osmanli conqueror Sultan Mehemet Fatih broke through it into the city.

It still constitutes the city boundary.

PLATE V OLD MECCA PILGRIM — HODJA

on the Golden Horn.

In this European quarter of the city stands the new Sultan's Palace

and looks across to neighbouring Asia.

94 THE OLD SARAY OF CONSTANTINOPLE

One of the many garden-palaces in the grounds of the Harem peninsula.

95 SARAY-BURNU

A section of the old Saray.

96 INNER QUARTERS OF THE OLD SARAY

Living-room and bedchamber of the Osman Sultan Murad III.

97 INNER QUARTERS OF THE PAVILION OF MUSTAFA PASHA
in the old Saray.

98 TOPKAP-SARAY

Old well in the palace yard of the old Saray.

99 ROCOCO WRITING-TABLE IN THE TOPKAP-SARAY MUSEUM

On the rear side of the little cupboard there is a painting

showing a general view of the Saray of those days.

ANATOLIA —
LAND AND PEOPLE

101 GREEK SCULPTURE

from the Museum in Smyrna-Izmir. Lion Frieze.

100 ROW OF COLUMNS ON THE ANCIENT AGORA

Market square in Smyrna-Izmir.

103 POSEIDON AND DEMETER

The Ocean God and the Goddess of Fertility used probably to stand upon an altar

in the Agora in Smyrna in Marcus Aurelius's day (A.D. 121—180). In the present-day Agora Museum in Izmir.

102 TOMB-STONES OF OSMAN NOTABILITIES

from the Museum in Izmir.

104 GREEK SCULPTURES

Frieze on the Aegean shore.

105 POSEIDON OF SMYRNA

Magnificent head of the Greek Ocean God in white marble.

106 Entrance to the Amphitheatre of Side on the Mediterranean

The ancient city lay on the bay of Antalya (Attalea).

107 THE AMPHITHEATRE OF SIDE

had accommodation for 13,000 persons and, despite earthquake damage, is still most impressive.

109   Seljuk Minaret in Antalya

108   This Waterfall near Antalya drops nearly one hundred feet

Thousands of streams flow through the fertile valley of Antalya

to empty themselves into the Mediterranean.

110 WATERFALLS NEAR MANAVGAT

111 THE PRESENT-DAY HARBOUR OF ANTALYA
     the ancient Attalea, on the Mediterranean. The best harbour in outhern Anatolia,
     but without connection by land.

PLATE VI ASPENDOS NEAR ANTALYA
     One of the best preserved amphitheatres. Built by Zenone during the reign of the Roman
     Emperor Antoninus Pius (138—61).

112 SELJUK MOSQUE IN ANTALYA (ATTALEA)

a reconstructed Early Christian church, now a museum.

113 LYCIAN STONE PLINTH

Carving from the region around Xanthus.

115 VIEW OF ANTALYA

   showing Hadrian's Arch, which has now sunk well into the ground.

114 TRIUMPHAL ARCH IN ANTALYA (ATTALEA)

   built in honour of the Emperor Hadrian (A.D. 117—138).

116 DETAIL OF HADRIAN'S ARCH

The original height of the archway was 26 feet. It is built entirely of white marble.

117 LION AT THE ENTRANCE TO THE GRAND TOWN PARK OF ANTALYA

119 On the Castle Hill in Alanya

118 Alanya on the Mediterranean seen from the Castle Hill

120 PORTION OF THE BYZANTINE CASTLE OF SILIFKE

Seleucus Nicator founded the ancient Seleucia, present-day Silifke, around 300 B.C.

121 ROMAN BRIDGE OVER THE GÖKSU

the ancient Calycadnus, in the waters of which the Emperor Frederick Barbarossa

was drowned in 1190 during the third Crusade.

123 YOUNG CAMEL IN SILIFKE

At a height of some 4,600 feet these dromedaries are very valuable servants of man.

122 WHITE TURBE — A SMALL MAUSOLEUM IN SILIFKE

124–125 CORYCUS AND THE ALMOST LEGENDARY ISLAND OF KIZKALE —
THE MAIDEN'S CASTLE

the forgotten citadel of Antiquity on the riviera of Asia Minor
is an ancient royal residence near Mersin.

126 THE LAST REMAINS OF POMPEIOPOLIS

Pompey (106—48 B.C.) founded this town in the vicinity of the present-day Mersin.

127 CORINTHIAN CAPITAL FROM THE NEIGHBOURHOOD OF MERSIN ON THE MEDITERRANEAN COAST

128 THE MEDITERRANEAN SHORE AT MERSIN

Mersin is the fruit-garden of Asia Minor.

129 ROAD SCENE IN MERSIN

What the baby-carriage is for us — the donkey is here.

Mother and child on donkey-back are served by a Bakal (vendor).

130   The Ulu Cami or 'Great Mosque' in Tarsus

The town of St. Paul offers few remains from the ancient past.

This Seljuk mosque dates from the eleventh to the twelfth centuries.

131   Interior of the Ulu Cami

The muezzin at prayer. Beneath him lies buried the son of Harun-el-Rashid.

Plate vii   Büyük Ada — The Big Island — formerly Principo

As early as Byzantine times these wooded islands in the ancient Propontis were
favourite health resorts.

132 MINBER — THE MOHAMMEDAN PULPIT

in the giant mosque.

134 THE THERMAE OF HIEROPOLIS

originally a city of priests. Phrygian foundation.

Enlarged in the second century B.C. by Eumenus II, King of Pergamum.

135 WATER-BUFFALOES AT THE SITE OF THE BIBLICAL LAODICEA

in the background lies Hieropolis with the sinter terraces of the 'Cotton-wool Castle'.

136–137 STALACTITE DEPOSITS OF THE 'COTTON-WOOL CASTLE'

These terraces, over which hot water flows, have the appearance of icebergs.

138–139 TYPICAL ANATOLIAN LANDSCAPE AT BURDUR

The yellowish colouring of the earth is characteristic.

140–141 Carpet weavers from Isparta

The old designs are highly valued.

142 PEASANT'S CART ON THE FIELDS AT BURDUR

it could be the original vehicle of the Hittites.

143 IN THE HIGH PLATEAUX OF ASIA MINOR

Goats and sheep — the Turks' basic possessions — seek their sparse

fodder in the often deeply cleft valleys of Anatolia.

144 SOUTH-WEST ANATOLIAN VILLAGE SCENE NEAR BURDUR

The characteristic flat-roofed type of building is found all over Asia Minor.

145 THE VILLAGE OF ERENCIKÖY IN CENTRAL ANATOLIA
still evinces a Hittite style of building.

146 Ararat — the highest Mountain in Asia Minor

with its 16,916 feet it constitutes an arresting landmark on the Russian frontier of Turkey.

Plate viii Pamukkale near Hierapolis

The 'Cotton-wool Castle' is what the Turks call the stalactitic deposits

of the Cürük su, the ancient Likos.

147 Bridge across the Euphrat

148 View of the Old Town of Ankara with Atatürk's Mausoleum

149 THE MAUSOLEUM OF THE 'FATHER OF TURKEY'
Kemal Atatürk.

150 THE MUSEUM OF ETHNOGRAPHY IN ANKARA

151 INTERIOR OF THE MAUSOLEUM CONTAINING ATATÜRK'S SARCOPHAGUS IN ANKARA

152 ANKARA'S CITADEL, THE ANCIENT ANCYRA, WITH THE OLD TOWN

153 Statue of Atatürk in front of the Museum of Ethnography in Ankara with Sumerian stone lion

154 Roadway in Ankara's Citadel

155 OLD MINARET IN THE OLD TOWN OF ANKARA

156 THE 'TRUST MEMORIAL' IN THE NEW TOWN OF ANKARA:

Learn, work, trust, — saying of Atatürk.

157 SUMERIAN LION OUTSIDE THE MUSEUM OF ETHNOGRAPHY IN ANKARA

159 MODERN PLEASURE-GRAND IN THE CENTRE OF ANKARA

The large Youth Park with the Opera House in the background.

158 THE ROMANTIC PIRATES' FORT OF ANAMUR

on the western shores of the Mediterranean — opposite Cyprus.

160 ISLANDS IN THE SEA OF MARMARA

as seen from Asia Minor.

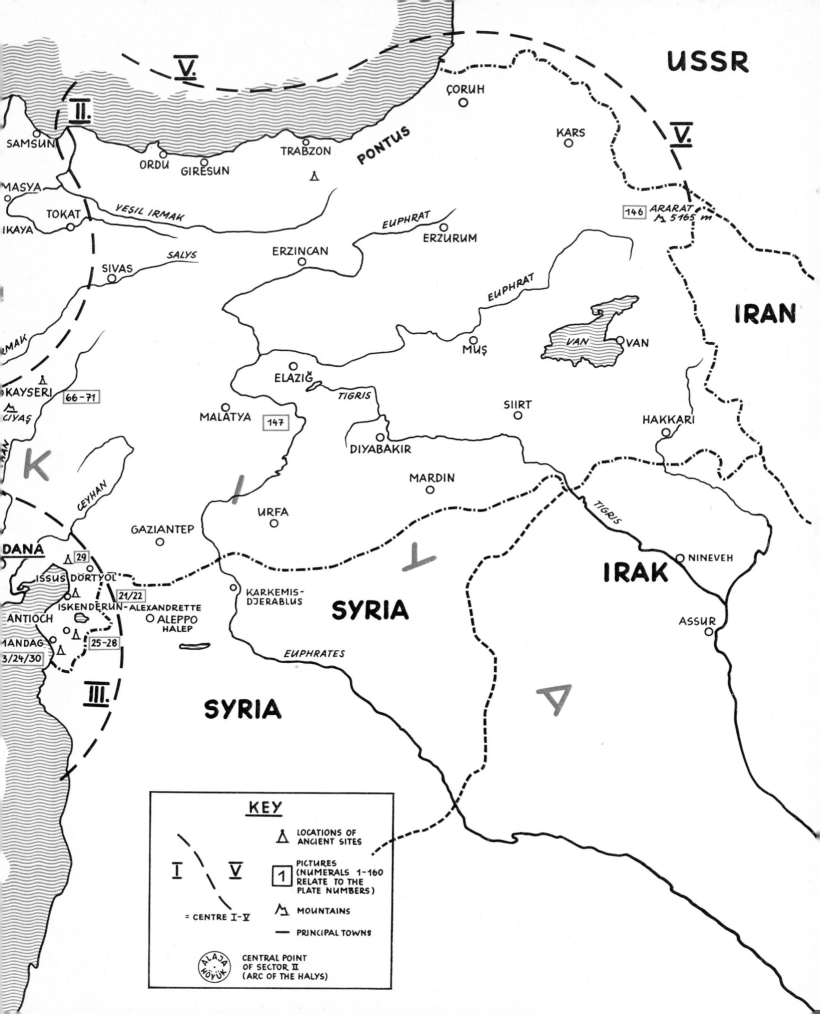

USSR

$\overline{V}$.

$\overline{II}$.

SAMSUN

ORDU
GIRESUN

ÇORUH

TRABZON   PONTUS

KARS

$\overline{V}$.

MASYA

TOKAT

YEŞIL IRMAK

IKAYA

SALYS

SIVAS

ERZINCAN

EUPHRAT

ERZURUM

146 ARARAT
△ 5165 m

IRAN

rMAK

KAYSERI

66-71

CIYAŞ

K

ELAZIĞ

MALATYA

147

TIGRIS

EUPHRAT

MUŞ

VAN

VAN

SIIRT

HAKKARI

DIYABAKIR

CEYHAN

DANA

29

ISSUS DÖRTYOL

ISKENDERUN-ALEXANDRETTE

21/22

ANTIOCH

ALEPPO
HALEP

MANDAG

25-28

3/24/30

$\overline{III}$.

GAZIANTEP

URFA

MARDIN

KARKEMIS-
DJERABLUS

SYRIA

⊥

TIGRIS

IRAK

NINEVEH

ASSUR

SYRIA

EUPHRATES

▽

KEY

△ LOCATIONS OF
    ANCIENT SITES

$\overline{I}$ $\overline{V}$

1 PICTURES
    (NUMERALS 1-160
    RELATE TO THE
    PLATE NUMBERS)

= CENTRE $\overline{I}$-$\overline{V}$

⩕ MOUNTAINS

— PRINCIPAL TOWNS

ALAJA
HÖYÜK

CENTRAL POINT
OF SECTOR $\overline{II}$
(ARC OF THE HALYS)